S0-DFI-681

Comrades of the Trail

Comrades of the Trail

Josh and his part-wolf dog race the winter storms to drive his family's herd of cattle across the mountains. Can they do it by themselves?

Colleen L. Reece

Tillamook, Oregon

0058

REVIEW AND HERALD PUBLISHING ASSOCIATION
Washington, DC 20039-0555
Hagerstown, MD 21740

Copyright © 1986 by
Review and Herald Publishing Association

This book was
Edited by Gerald Wheeler
Designed by Richard Steadham
Cover art by Walt Sturrock
Type set:11/12 Zapf

PRINTED IN U.S.A.

R&H Cataloging Service

Reece, Colleen Loraine, 1935-
    Comrades of the trail.

    I. Title.
        818.54

ISBN 0-8280-0355-6

DEDICATION

For my nephew David, who loves dogs.

Wolf

A deep growl in his throat, the huge white dog strained against the frayed rope holding him prisoner. Suddenly a mighty lunge snapped it in two.

"Hold, there!" The angry man looming above him swung the whip that had already left welts on the dog's sides. It lashed and fell, and with it came another yelp of pain.

"*You* hold there!" Twelve-year-old Josh Kincaid grabbed the man's gnarled wrist with skinny fingers that clutched like eagle talons. His brown eyes that matched his hair blazed and the freckles stood out like rust spots on his flushed face. "What kind of man are you to beat your dog?"

"Get away, brat." The man shook the boy the way a cat does a mouse. "He's not my dog. He's a cur, quarter-strain wolf, I hear tell." Although he flung Josh aside, the boy would not give up. Even as the bearded homesteader lifted the whip again, Josh threw himself down in front of the panting dog.

"Get out of there!" Anger changed to alarm. "He'll kill you."

For a single instant paralyzing fear shot through the boy. He glanced behind him into bloodshot eyes. Had he gotten himself into another mess by his defense of the wounded animal?

The dog snarled, then inched closer, crawling on his belly.

Slowly Josh put out one hand, hating the way it trembled, but knowing it would be useless to try and run if the dog really was a killer.

Another low growl began deep in the dog's throat. It rumbled through Josh like thunder, but he still held out his hand.

Never taking his eyes off the boy, the animal continued to creep toward him. Inches from the outstretched hand he sniffed. Growled again. Then with a tired sigh he rested his nose on the dirty brown hand.

Shoulders heaving, Josh slumped.

"Well, I'll be . . ." The giant above them took one step closer, peering in shock.

"Get back!" Josh's warning whisper mingled with more snarls. The white beast showed his wolf heritage. Every hair bristled.

The homesteader backed off, hate showing in every muscle. "You interferin' whelp. If ever I get you away from him you'll get the same as he got." He twisted the whip. The dog crouched for attack, but Josh held him firmly.

A crisp, authoritative voice cut the sunny autumn air. "That's about enough, Sievers. Get off my land."

"Kincaid!" The man with the whip spun around and glared at the tall man whose mahogany hair and eyes were so like his son's. "Your land for three days more, remember." Menace filled every word. "Then it's mine."

"More's the pity. I wish now I'd never sold to you."

Triumph gleamed in the faded blue eyes. The twisted mouth spat tobacco juice that left a dirty dribble down one side of the leathery cheek. "That's your affair. Just be sure you're out." He shot a venomous look at Josh and the dog. "An' take that wolf-dog with you. Utah don't want him. Wyomin' probably won't, neither." Sievers mounted his mule and dug his heels into the animal's sides. "Three days, you hear?"

Jacob Kincaid didn't bother to answer. "All right, son, what's it about?"

Relief flooded Josh. "Aw, Pa, he was beating the dog and—"

"And you couldn't stand it." A smile curled around his father's lips. It gave way to concern when he got a full view of the size of the dog. "Didn't you think that dog might be dangerous?"

Josh hung his head. It wasn't the first time he'd acted without thinking. "Guess not. But he likes me now." The boy ran one hand over the matted hair, so thick it felt like fur. "He can go to Wyoming with us, like Mr. Sievers said."

A frown crossed Mr. Kincaid's face. "I don't know about that. If he's really part wolf . . ." He left the sentence unfinished. "First, we've got to get him fixed up. Those cuts will heal once they're washed."

It took a full hour for Josh to persuade Wolf, as he named his new dog, to let Pa doctor him, but once it was over the dog lay down on the hearth before the crackling fire and closed his eyes.

"We've work to do, son," the man reminded his son. "Like Sievers said, we've only got three days to get out of here." He sighed. "It's late in the year to start across the Wasatch Mountains. Those 130 miles to the Salt River valley aren't going to be easy."

Josh glanced out the open door of their log cabin. Already white streaked the top of the mountains. "We can make it, Pa. Good thing Ma and Sam and the girls went ahead with the wagons."

"Maybe I should have sent you with them," Pa speculated. "But you wanted so much to go with the herd."

"You won't be sorry," Josh promised, feeling bad over the times he'd let his father down. "Those 25 head of cattle will hardly know we're moving, I'll treat them so good."

"If Siever had paid when he was supposed to, we wouldn't have had to wait until the first of October." His gaze followed Josh's. "Well, we'll just have to pray for good weather. We'll take it easy, about 15 miles a day, and be there in a little over a week."

"Will we travel on the Sabbath?"

"No. Jesus talked about pulling an ox from a pit on the Sabbath but," Pa's eyes twinkled. "If the ox falls into a pit *every* Sabbath, you'd better either sell the ox or fill in the pit! We will carefully make plans so we won't have to travel on the Sabbath. Both man and beast need the rest, as well as to keep the day holy."

Josh laughed so hard at Pa that Wolf opened one sleepy eye, then settled back down. "I'm glad we're going to Wyoming. Even though it's beautiful here," he said, looking out at the golden aspens and gently rolling hills dotted with pine and spruce. He could hardly wait to make the trail drive, his first. His 15-year-old brother Sam had gone when they had made a drive a few years ago. Now it was his turn, and he vowed to make his father proud.

Two days later he and Pa were doing a final check of

the cattle and getting them ready to move. Suddenly his father's horse, Daisy, hit a gopher hole, stumbled, and threw Pa.

"Pa, Pa!" Josh screamed, sliding from big black Ebony's back and racing to his father.

"I'm all right." Mr. Kincaid raised on one elbow, then collapsed back to the hard ground. "Oh, no. I think I broke a couple ribs." Sweat beaded on his pale face. "Ride for John Tanner."

Josh leaped on the horse. "Fly, Ebony."

The three miles to their nearest neighbor's place flashed by in a blur. Then the boy pounded at the door. "Mr. Tanner, Pa's hurt. He says it's busted ribs."

The man started for his tumbledown barn. "I better take a wagon. Your folks're all gone, aren't they?"

"Yeah. Just me left." The words floated back over Josh's shoulder. Ebony already headed cross country, leaving Mr. Tanner to follow.

" 'Pears there's two ribs cracked, Jacob," Mr. Tanner told them after he gently probed and pushed, forcing an "aghh" of pain from Mr. Kincaid. He rocked back on his heels. "You'll be good as new in a few weeks."

"A few weeks!" Pa tried to sit up but fell back. "We have to be out of here tomorrow."

"Impossible." Mr. Tanner shook his graying head. "You can't ride with cracked ribs—not for a couple weeks at the very least." Hope flickered in his eyes. "Sure, Sievers'll let you stay, what with the accident and all."

"He might have, three days ago."

Josh squirmed. Was his defense of Wolf going to make more trouble?

"Josh caught Sievers beating a stray dog. He interfered," Pa explained, sending a sickly grin toward

11

his son. "I wouldn't have had him do different, but Sievers won't be willing to give us an extra hour, let alone more."

"Well, I'm taking you in the wagon to our place for tonight," Mr. Tanner said. He struggled to get up and motioned Josh to help him.

"There's too much to do," Pa protested. "I tell you, we have to get out of here tomorrow."

"Look here, Jacob." Josh had never heard Mr. Tanner sound so stern. "Cracked ribs aren't something you can mess with. I don't think there's any broken bone fragments that could puncture your lung, but you can't take a chance. You and Josh can stay with us until you're ready to ride."

The generous offer didn't lighten Pa's despair. "We've got to get those cattle across the Salt River range before snow flies. The pass is over 7,600 feet high and tomorrow's October 1. You know what that means." He looked straight into Tanner's face.

"Reckon I do," the old man admitted. "But what choice do you have? No," he silenced Pa. "Right now we're getting you where I can look you over better." He waved at the already setting sun that sat on the rim of a distant purple hill like a button on a cap. "Can't half see out here."

Mr. Kincaid didn't say any more, just tried to help as Mr. Tanner and Josh lifted him into the wagon.

"I'll stay here tonight," Josh volunteered. "I can make sure everything's done so tomorrow—" he choked off. What would tomorrow bring?

"Sure you'll be all right?"

Feeling smaller than he was, Josh stood up straight. "Yeah. Besides"—his hand dropped to Wolf's shaggy head, which was clean now, from the bath and brushing the boy had coaxed him into the day before—"Wolf will look after me."

Pa relaxed a bit. "Thank God! That dog's followed Josh like a shadow ever since he brought him home," he told Mr. Tanner. "Well, if you're sure you're all right . . ."

"I am, Pa." Josh tried to stretch even taller.

"You come over first thing in the morning so we can figure out what to do."

"I will." The boy and dog watched the creaking wagon go out of sight. Then, "Come on, Wolf, we have to count the cattle." He mounted Ebony again and the dog trotted alongside. It didn't take long. Josh and his father had rounded them up and put them in a rude wire pen just that morning. To their amazement, Wolf had helped—barking and racing after half-grown calves who showed signs of wanting to escape.

The cabin had never been so empty and still before. Little pieces of their life in Utah lay scattered about: Sam's extra handkerchief, 4-year-old Mercy's doll, Ma's apron. The room was barren except for the built-in bunks and the few quilts and clothes left behind. What would their home in Wyoming be like? Suddenly an avalanche of loneliness swept over him. What was his family doing right now? They should have reached their destination a week ago. Was his twin sister Charity looking out the widow of a different house, staring south and west, missing him the way he was missing her? Charity was better than another boy. They had great times together. Sam always teased Josh about the special friendship he had with his twin, but the boy didn't care. There wasn't any way to tell Sam or anybody else that Charity was part of him. When she wasn't around, he felt as if a chunk of himself was actually missing.

A pounding at the door roused him. Who was here at this time of night? Wolf growled once, twice, then fell silent. "Who is it?"

"Sievers."

In a flash Wolf reached the locked door, frantically pawing to get at his enemy.

What did that crook want? Josh wondered with disgust. The boy had never heard his father say he'd been cheated on the price of the place, but he had his own idea. Now he wouldn't tell Sievers about the accident and see him gloat.

Josh flung back a shutter from a window. "Wolf won't let you in. What do you want?" He tried to sound as brave as he could.

"Jest lookin' round *my* property."

"It's not yours yet, so get off our land!"

An evil leer from the dim face in the shadows followed a muttered curse. "When you go, make sure everythin's left that's s'posed to be, or I'll have the sheriff on you."

Josh slammed the shutter shut, but it didn't close out the man's cackle. Wolf barked again. Rage stirred in Josh. How did that—that *dog-beater* dare say such a thing? Pa lived by the big Bible that always lay open on the mantel. His word was as good as an oath.

It took Josh a long time to settle down again under his blankets with Wolf by his bunk. The blacker the night grew, the darker his thoughts. He tried to pray, but God seemed far away, not close like when the others were home and Pa read from the Bible and Ma told them stories. What would Daniel or Moses or Peter do?

Finally Josh fell into a sleep troubled by threatening

men with whips and bawling cattle. He woke to find pale streaks of morning sneaking in around the edges of the shutters. If only he could help Pa.

Then like a bolt of lightning an idea came. He gasped, felt his heart pound, and leaped from the bunk. Wolf came alive and bounded up beside him. The wild thought filled every muscle and bone of his body.

"I'll do it! I'll help Pa!" He scurried into his clothes, grabbed a leftover biscuit and an apple, and saddled Ebony. Ten minutes later he was streaking toward the Tanner place, followed by his excited dog.

A Big Job

Mr. Tanner was just leaving the barn, foaming milk buckets in both hands.

"Where's Pa? Is he all right?" Josh demanded.

"He's fine." Mr. Tanner's worn face crinkled into a smile. "Reckon when your pa tells you to get here early, you listen."

The quiet answer calmed the boy for a moment. He followed the old man up on the porch. "Is he awake yet?"

"Certainly. Jacob Kincaid isn't one to lie abed when there's things to be decided."

Josh hesitated. A faint understanding of what Pa faced crept into his brain. The next instant Mr. Tanner set down his buckets on the bench and opened the rude door. "Here's Josh, everyone." His eyes twinkled. "I put in mind he probably hasn't had breakfast."

Josh was vaguely aware of Mrs. Tanner and three barefoot children greeting him. He could smell flapjacks and warm syrup. Then his eyes riveted on his father, pale, but propped against two pillows on a low cot across the room.

"Pa," his voice shook. "You don't have to worry anymore." He swallowed hard.

"Why's that?" His father looked him square in the face.

"I'm going to drive the cattle to Wyoming."

The silence was so great Josh could hear the sizzle of grease in the pan on the stove clear across the room.

He swallowed again. "Pa, didn't you hear me?" His voice grew louder, more determined. "I am taking the herd to Wyoming—today!" He didn't give his father a chance to reply but rushed on. "Mr. Sievers came last night after dark. I didn't tell him you'd been hurt. I just kept still and let him rave. He acted like he already owned the place and made a bunch of rotten remarks about us taking off with stuff that was supposed to be left. I slammed the shutter on him after saying it wasn't his place until today. Oh, Pa, we've just got to get out before he comes back! He's a horrible person. Wolf would have got him for sure, but I didn't open the door." He was almost out of breath. "So, soon as I can, I'm getting the herd and starting out. I'll bring Daisy here, and when you're ready to ride you can come. It won't take you near as long without a herd." He clenched his hands until the nails bit into his palms. "Please, Pa, can I?"

Josh could feel his face get hot in the eternity of silence that followed his outburst. Why hadn't he come in and explained it all reasonably instead of blurting everything out? Probably that killed any chance he had of going. He was almost afraid to look at his father. If Pa once shook his head No it was all over. He wouldn't change his mind.

Well, he had to know. He stared at his father, noticing how still he lay, waiting for Josh to finish. The Tanners stood openmouthed around the room. The flapjacks lay cooling on the big platter on the table.

Josh's heart beat in his ears. Would Pa never speak?

Minutes or hours later—the boy wasn't sure which—Mr. Kincaid quietly said, "Do you know what such a trip will mean?"

"I—I think so." He'd actually not gone much past deciding it was the only thing they could do. His mind settled and began to work right again. "It means being responsible for the cattle and Ebony and Wolf. It means doing whatever's necessary to get there."

A little smile crossed Pa's haggard face. "Josh, you've said it. You'll be steward over the animals."

"Steward? Isn't that something they had in the Bible a lot?" Josh tried to remember.

"Yes. The actual meaning in the Old Testament was someone who was so close to the master of the property that he could know just what to do and how to do it the way the master would. He was in charge in the master's absence."

The enormity of the job ahead hit the boy right between the eyes. "You mean I have to fill your boots? Oh, Pa, I could never do that!" The next moment he bit his lip. Why had he said such a thing, even if it was true? "But I can try," he added. "If I just ask myself what you'd do if you were there, I can do it. I know I can."

"I believe you can too, Josh. You've punched cows since you could ride, and that was just after you learned to walk." The injured man's eyes softened.

"That's right," Josh agreed eagerly. "Wolf and Ebony are smart. They can help me a lot."

A growing light in Pa's eyes stopped Josh. "You'll have another comrade of the trail, Josh. God is just as much out in those mountains and valleys He created as He is here."

A funny feeling swept through the boy. "Uh, yeah."

He dug his toe in the hand-braided rug on the board floor. Slowly confidence crept through him. "Shall I go get the herd and what little's left at the cabin?"

"Not until after breakfast," Mrs. Tanner spoke for the first time. "You sit yourself down and wrap yourself around those flapjacks." She poured milk from an old pitcher. One of the children must have filled it from the buckets outside, Josh thought. It was still warm from the cow. Gladly he stuffed himself. "I won't be getting this kind of cooking out on the trail," he told her and received a warm smile in return.

"I'll pack a few extras to go with the flour and beans and things you've already got," she told him. "Apples are good for you and don't take up much room. You've got rice and salt and what you need?"

"Yes, ma'am. Pa and I packed it yesterday." Josh wiped his mouth on his shirt sleeve and got up. "I thank you." He turned to his father. "I'll be back soon."

This time he didn't race Ebony home. Since it was a long way to Wyoming, he wasn't about to start out with a tired horse.

It didn't take long to remove their few remaining belongings from the cabin. Josh hesitated, then set his jaw and swept the floor. "I'm not doing it for old man Sievers," he told Wolf, who growled in agreement. "Ma'd want it done." Carefully he latched the door and didn't look back. No sense brooding over leaving. He had a long way to go and a man-sized job to do. Yet after he rounded up the herd and got them started in an orderly way, he reined in his horse at the top of the knoll and glanced back—once.

When he reached the Tanners, their old friend directed, "Leave the cattle by the stream. They won't go anywhere. Your Pa wants you before you take off. You can spend the night and start tomorrow, if you want."

Josh shook his head. "I can get in maybe 10 miles before dark. As Pa said, this time of year a body'd better make tracks while he can." He stepped inside the Tanner cabin.

His father beckoned him over to the bed. He had a slab of wood on his lap for a writing desk and a piece of paper marked with a stubby pencil. "I've made a map. It's crude, but it will get you on the right track. Whatever you do, don't lose it. Keep it in your shirt pocket. I doubt that you'll find many people on the trail. Maybe no one. You need this to go by. If for any reason you get in a tight spot and do lose it, use the North Star by night and the sun by day."

He pointed at the map. "See? Now, there's plenty of water so you shouldn't have trouble finding that, once you get to Bear Lake. Between here and there it may be pretty dry. Water the cattle, all they can drink, before you go. Don't push them too hard. Let them walk, but keep them moving. You can cover a lot of miles a day with a slow, steady pace. Give them time to graze their fill night and morning and rest them often."

Josh looked curiously at the map. The immensity of the job ahead finally sank in. First he'd been excited over helping Pa, then over being in charge. Now he eyed the wavy line he was to follow. That little line represented dark, lonely nights, dusty days, and lurking dangers. He shivered and studied what Pa had drawn.

"I'll be in three states, huh, Pa?"

"That's right." Pa traced the route. "You won't hit much of Idaho, just 'cross the southeast corner. There will be some empty country south of Montpelier. You don't get that far north. Instead you'll turn off near the lower end of Bear Lake."

Shivers ran through the boy, to be replaced by pride at his father's matter-of-fact way of talking. But Pa wasn't through. He told Josh, "Bring in the big Bible from your saddlebag. I don't know how Ma missed it when she loaded everything up, but she did." He raised his voice. "Can all you Tanners come in for a few minutes?"

Josh stole a look at Pa's solemn face then went for the Bible.

"This boy of mine's heading out on a big job. He's prepared as far as food, a map, and determination. Now we need to make sure he's really prepared. It's a long, hard trek to Wyoming and Josh is going to need all the help he can get." Flipping open the Bible, Pa turned to the twenty-third psalm. " 'The Lord is my Shepherd . . .' " He read it all. Next he read different verses. " 'For every beast of the forest is mine, and the cattle upon a thousand hills' " (Psalm 50:10). " 'Our cattle also shall go with us; there shall not an hoof be left behind; for thereof must we take to serve the Lord our God; and we know not with what we must serve the Lord, until we come thither' " (Exodus 10:26).

At last he turned to the New Testament and Matthew 18:12. His voice grew rich and deep as he read the familiar story. " 'How think ye? if a man have an hundred sheep, and one of them be gone astray, doth he not leave the ninety and nine, and goeth into the mountains, and seeketh that which is gone astray?' "

Blinking hard, Josh lost the rest of the reading. His ears roared. Could he live up to what his father expected? He had to. He was the steward.

"Josh." There was a tone in Pa's voice the boy had never heard before. "You have taken on a great responsibility. Now we will ask that you receive help to fulfill it."

Hastily his son bowed his head. Pa's voice rolled over him, warming him the way the warm woolen coat Ma had made last winter did. "Our heavenly Father, we entrust this child to Thy care. We ask that Thou will grant strength, wisdom, and Thy loving protection to him. The road before him is long. The way will be steep and rocky. Yet, we know Thy Son trod a rough and rocky road for us all. We ask, therefore, a special blessing on Joshua, whose name was chosen because it meant 'Jehovah is salvation.' In Jesus' name and for His sake, Amen."

In the little pool of silence after the prayer Josh felt some of the heaviness fall away. How could he fail with a blessing like that? "Thanks, Pa."

A rare and beautiful smile passed between father and son. "I'll be with you soon. Probably just a few days after you get there."

"Good, Pa, but don't hurry too much." A sudden thought crossed his mind. "Did you want the Bible left here?"

"No. It goes back in your saddlebag."

Josh picked up the well-worn Black Book with its frayed edges. It had been part of his childhood. Now it would go with him as he took the first faltering steps into manhood. Even the feeling of it gave him courage.

"Oh, son—there's one more scripture." Pa leaned forward. "Nights around the campfire you might want to look up the ninety-first psalm, especially verse 5." A curious glint flashed in his eyes and he gripped Josh's hand with his own toilworn, calloused fingers. A bond of strength seemed to flow through the boy's wrist and into his system.

"Don't forget—Psalm 91:5."

"I won't, Pa." Hurrying out the door, Josh tucked the Bible safely in the saddlebag bulging with good things Mrs. Tanner had provided, and mounted Ebony. "Come on, Wolf. Get along, you critters, we're off for Wyoming."

The herd bellowed a bit, but obediently started up the trail. Josh's cattle drive had begun.

Terror
in the Night

J osh rounded the first bend from the Tanner cabin. Suddenly his high spirits demanded release. "Yah-hoo!" he hollered. The effect was instantaneous. Wolf howled. Ebony reared. The herd panicked. By the time Josh got the horse under control, the cattle were long gone down the dusty trail.

"Stupid dumbhead," he told himself in disgust. Wolf barked reproachfully and Ebony nickered. "Not you. Me," he reassured them and headed after his bellowing herd. Good thing he'd been out of sight. After a performance like that Pa would most likely decide he wasn't such a great trail driver and then where would they be?

"Hi-yi, get in there!" Josh chased the cattle, weaving in and out, then riding ahead and pointing the lead steer until he slowed.

It took a long time to get his charges settled down and marching up the trail in an orderly fashion. Wolf proved himself invaluable. Just let an ornery steer try to break rank and Wolf raced after him in a flash.

"I guess the sheepdog in you's more important than the wolf, old boy." Josh patted the rough head. The dog licked his hand, leaving it wet but tingling with friendship.

Ebony whinnied jealously. "You, too." Josh stroked the smooth neck. "You're both great trail comrades." He brushed a fly away from his sweaty face. "Pa said God'd be our comrade too. He doesn't have to prove Himself—but I wonder if we'll recognize . . ." The thought trailed off as a calf wandered away from its mother then set up a cry that almost awakened the sleeping mountains. By the time Josh herded it back he'd forgotten what he'd been musing about.

Herding hadn't been such hard work when Pa was around, Josh thought for the fiftieth time. The sleepy afternoon gave way to a chill in the air. Josh noticed the greedy fingers of winter were already starting to strip the aspens of their golden leaves. It was great swishing through the fallen leaves, a lot better than eating the dust of the trail. Much of the time Josh could herd the cattle alongside the regular trail, and the leaves softened the *pad-pad* of hooves. When the sun lit only the tops of the tall evergreens the boy knew it was time to stop. He chose to make camp on a rising bluff, away from any canyon.

"Never camp in a canyon," Pa had taught them since childhood. "Flash floods come roaring down with the force of a waterfall. They carry logs and the water can sweep away anything in its path." So Josh carefully selected a grassy, flat place. There was a pool of water nearby, small, but big enough to water the cattle. He bedded them down after allowing them a full graze, then began his own simple preparations.

"I never camped out without Pa or Sam before," he told Wolf. The big dog cocked one ear sympathetically. "Reckon I'll talk to you and Ebony so it won't be so lonesome." He measured out a portion of oats for the horse, then shook his head and put them back. "Old boy, you can graze instead. There's good grass here. We'll save the oats for later."

"Wow!" he said a few minutes later. "Would you look at this?"

Wolf not only looked; he licked his lips. Mrs. Tanner had put her time to good use. A sack of biscuits, corn bread, and a loaf of brown bread waited in the pack. Even an apple pie, a bit mashed, but delicious-looking.

"We won't have to cook tonight," Josh grinned. "Here's beans, too." He carefully lifted out a kettle of baked beans. "Now for a fire." There were plenty of pinecones around to make a hot fire. Once it blazed up, Josh let it die to a bed of coals. Then he made a strange kind of arrangement to toast his corn bread—setting strong sticks in the ground on each side of his fire and another across the forked ones. He hung his Dutch oven (pot) above the flames, heated the baked beans, then swished them out into a tin plate. Next he carefully cut pieces of corn bread and lay them in the hot pot until they were warmed through.

"Say, this is life," Josh said to himself. He tossed another bit of corn bread to Wolf. "One dish to wash. One pot. How come Charity makes such a big thing over doing dishes, anyway?" After he finished eating— he had decided to save at least half the apple pie for the next day—he scoured his Dutch oven and tin plate and fork with sand. They could dry next to the fire.

"Making a bed isn't all that hard, either," he told the dog. "Look." He chose a spot where the grass was rich and deep, away from the direction the smoke blew. "First we throw down a tarp [tarpaulin—big piece of canvas]. Then comes one blanket. I'll use my coat for a pillow." His trained hands worked as he talked,

27

spreading blankets, smoothing out wrinkles. "Another blanket, pull the tarp over the whole thing. Leave enough so if it rains we can reach down and bring the end over our heads, and—magic! Our bed's ready."

Wolf whimpered and inched closer.

"Yeah, you too. You can sleep with me."

The animal's tail beat a tattoo on the ground.

It was really dark now. The shadow of the nearby foothills rising to the mountains blocked out any light left. Josh mounted Ebony and rode around the cattle. They were quiet, lying down, settled for the night. Satisfaction filled him. He'd had a bad start, but so far everything else was fine. With a yawn he announced, "Time to turn in, Wolf." He slid from Ebony's bare back and carefully hobbled the animal. Not used to hobbles, the horse didn't like it, but Josh couldn't take a chance on him wandering away in the night. He'd unsaddled earlier and hadn't bothered to resaddle for the short cattle check.

The chores were over. The night was suddenly still, stiller than Josh could remember. What a great time they'd have if Charity were here! He forced himself to forget the blackness of the night. "Hey, Wolf, you'll like Charity. She'll probably spoil you since she's crazy about dogs and ours died a few months ago." His voice sounded small in the night. The fire flickered low. Uneasy thoughts crept through him. He felt for the small rifle his father had insisted he bring. Pa had said, "Remember, we don't hold with killing. This rifle's never to be fired except to save your life."

"Aw, I won't need it," Josh had answered. "Nothing's going to bother me."

"Probably not, but once in a great while an animal goes wild and attacks. Keep the rifle handy."

Now the boy's fingers tightened on the polished stock and cold barrel. Far in the distance a howling began. Wolf growled, deep in his throat. Josh's free hand felt the furlike hair rising. "It's OK, old boy; those wolves are a long way off."

The dog didn't act like he heard. On stealthy feet he slowly crossed to the edge of the dimly lit firelight circle. Josh froze. Was his newly aquired dog going to desert?

Wolf threw back his head and howled. It echoed across the valley they had left. The cattle turned and shifted nervously but didn't get up. Ebony neighed. In the distance a reply from the wolf or wolves sounded, then grew fainter. The boy didn't realize he was holding his breath until Wolf relaxed, then walked back to crouch by his side.

Letting his hand drop to the dog's head, Josh released his breath and gulped in air. "Hey, comrade, you scared me there."

Wolf just whined. But the next instant he leaped to his feet barking furiously. A twig snapped, then another. Josh felt the hair on his neck rise the way Wolf's had done earlier.

Something was out there in the darkness.

Fear pumped through the boy. What if Sievers had followed him? He wouldn't put it past him to even steal the cattle. Rumors had spread about him, and Josh wasn't sure they were only rumors.

"What is it, Wolf?" he whispered. Should he cock the rifle? No. If it was a man the rifle might scare him, but it could go off, too. Josh shuddered. He would never, ever kill, no matter how backed to the wall he got. He didn't think he could even kill a bear or wolf unless it was the only way out, like Pa said.

29

Wolf remained in attack position, but Josh wound his hands in the long fur and warned, "Don't move."

The low brush just out of sight from the dying fire moved. Again. Wolf and Josh crouched silent as stone. Then something chuckled, sending relief through Josh. Wolf's rigid stance dropped.

"A porcupine! All that excitement for a silly porcupine!" Josh felt his knees buckle. The fat old porcupine rustled and waddled its way across the edge of the clearing, still grunting its weird sound into the forest.

"So old Quill-Thrower gave us the shakes." Josh almost rolled on the ground. Finally he stopped laughing and wiped his eyes. "You know he doesn't really throw his quills. He just gets into a prickly curled up ball and those needle-sharp quills stick in anything brushing against him."

Wolf eyed the boy disdainfully as if to say that *his* job was to warn of anything coming near camp, and Josh quit laughing. "We can't let fear stop us." He groped for the saddlebags and took out the Bible. Tossing another cone on the dying fire, he waited until it burned bright, then added two more, just enough to read by. "Pa said the ninety-first psalm." His quick fingers found the place and he held up the Book. One lock of reddish hair dangled in front of his eyes and he pushed it back, then read aloud.

" 'He that dwelleth in the secret place of the most High shall abide under the shadow of the Almighty. I will say of the Lord, He is my refuge and my fortress.' Hey, Wolf, pretty neat, huh? Refuge and fortress." He went on: " '. . . my God; in him will I trust. Surely he shall deliver thee from the snare of the fowler, and from the noisome pestilence—' How's that for a good name for old Quill-Thrower? Let's call him Noisome Pestilence. He's a pest, all right!"

Wolf didn't even grunt, just fixed his amber eyes on Josh and listened.

"'He shall cover thee with his feathers, and under his wings shalt thou trust: his truth shall be thy shield and buckler.' Oh, here's verse 5, the one Pa said to be sure and pay attention to: 'Thou shalt not be afraid for the terror by night; nor for the arrow that flieth by day; nor for the pestilence that walketh in darkness . . .'" His gaze skipped down to the following verses, then back to verse 5. "'Thou shalt not be afraid for the terror by night . . .' That's us, Wolf. We don't have to be scared." His rapidly beating heart slowed back to normal. He started to fit the Bible back into the saddlebag. Something white fluttered to the ground.

"What's this, Wolf?"

The dog edged closer.

Josh snatched the paper. "Hey, it's a letter from Pa. He must have had it ready and sneaked it in the Bible when he was reading." The boy spread the folded paper. "Let's see what he wrote." It was hard to read by the now-dim campfire, but Josh didn't want to build it up again. The forest was dry and he'd take no chances with fire. As he squinted, Pa's bold black writing stood out on the page:

"Dear Son,

"Whenever you read this passage it will be because something has happened to frighten you or because you are feeling the loneliness of the trail. Remember, even Wolf and the rifle are not the protectors you need. God is. He can and will meet every need.

"You might have forgotten a little story about your grandfather. When he was a young man he joined the

31

westward movement in the growing desire to have land for himself. It was in the days of Indians and warpaths. Your grandfather Kincaid scorned weapons.

"One day while he was plowing his field two Indians appeared. They asked for food. He brought it. They asked for flour and salt. He gave it to them freely.

"Then the older one, hideously painted, demanded, 'Gun. Knife.'

" 'I have no gun,' Grandfather said quietly. 'And the only knives I have are here.' He showed them a brush knife used for clearing and the table knives.

" 'White man fool,' the younger Indian taunted. 'He no have weapons.'

" 'I have a weapon,' Grandfather told them. The Indians were immediately on the alert. Their hands crept toward their hatchets and scalping knives.

" 'Where your weapon?' The older Indian leaped close and glared into Grandfather's face.

" 'Here.' Grandfather pointed to his heart.

"The young brave shot his hand inside Grandfather's faded homespun shirt. 'Nothing here. You crazy, white man?'

"Grandfather shook his head. 'No. My weapon is prayer.'

"The brave jumped back as if shot, but the old warrior said, 'Heap good weapon.' The next moment he swung the supplies he'd been given over one naked shoulder, motioned to the young brave, and slipped out of the door."

It was signed: Pa.

For a long time Josh didn't move. He could hear Ebony's soft breathing, smell wood smoke. He raised his head and stared up at the sky. The stars looked

32

close enough to pick. Pa's story sank deep into his heart.

Wolf shifted and Josh glanced down at him. Then he folded the letter, placed it in the Bible to mark the ninety-first psalm, and headed for bed. But long after Wolf lay snoring beside him, Josh lay still, watching the stars, feeling God's presence in the strangely friendly darkness.

Flash Flood

Josh opened his eyes to a frosty world. The sun wasn't yet up but daylight showed gray around him. Everything was white—grass, trees, even the tarp he'd pulled over him during the night. "Hey, Wolf, you're better than a hot brick." He curled closer to the dog. The animal opened one eye, sighed, and went back to sleep.

The boy laughed. "Good idea—we'll wait until the sun comes up before getting breakfast." But Josh couldn't get back to sleep. The fears of the night before faded with morning, and he could feel pride growing. He had actually spent the night alone in the foothills! Now he watched the first tinge of rose in the sky, then streaks of red, followed by angry orange before the sun came up. "Uh, oh—we may be in for a storm. The Bible even says a red morning sky means a storm." Jumping from the blankets, he pulled on his boots. "Glad I don't have to dress. Sleeping in clothes is the only way to sleep out here." By the time he got into his boots and warm jacket and had a fire started, his ears tingled and his hands were numb.

"Would you look at this?" Josh's mouth fell open. "Ice in the waterhole!" A thin sheet of ice around the edge of the pool showed pale gray. "Boy, we better make tracks while we can." Doubt stirred in him. Even Pa and Mr. Tanner hadn't expected a storm so soon. Would he be smart to turn the cattle and hightail it back?

"No!" He slammed down a frying pan with such force Wolf barked and jumped back. "I said we'd go through, and we will." Some of the tension dropped away and he hastily fried eggs, warmed leftover corn bread, and made a sort of sandwich to carry for the trail. If they were going to get caught in a storm, it could at least be a lot of miles farther on.

All day Josh rode with one eye on the cattle, the other on the scowling sky. The beauty of the strange sunrise threatened to fulfill its promise. By noon it gave way to grayness, and a light drizzle set in. The cattle seemed a little on edge, but made no trouble, just plodded ahead with Wolf and Josh and Ebony guiding them. "Glad there's a clear trail," Josh sighed with relief. "It'd be horrible to get out here and miss the way."

The rain let up late in the afternoon, but breaks in the clouds were not reassuring. Blood-red streaks mingled with the gray, and distant thunder rumbled over the hills. The wind had risen, and long before sunset Josh knew he'd have to find some kind of shelter. He let his gaze roam ahead. "Not the canyon. Too dangerous. Not the slope. The soft dirt could start the rocks above sliding." Finally he announced, "We'll stop there, Wolf."

"There" was another grassy pasture, but without the pool. "It will be a dry camp," Josh laughed out loud. "Well, dry as far as drinking water for the cattle! I've got a hunch—" The wind snatched his words away.

"All right, critters, get in there." He drove the herd

close together into the small meadow. They seemed glad enough to huddle in a bunch, although one could have heard their bawling clear to Wyoming.

Having forgotten to unwrap his slicker again after the drizzle stopped, Josh was soaked through before he got the cattle bedded down. Then there wasn't time before it started pouring again. Never had a fire felt so good as when he slowly turned before it, close enough to hear the sizzle of wet clothes drying and to lose his chill. He mustn't take cold or anything.

"At least we sleep in style tonight," Josh gloated. "See those two trees over there?" Wolf followed the pointing finger. "We'll just toss my lariat between them, throw the extra tarp over them, and peg them down with the wooden stakes Pa sent." After pounding down the stakes, he soon had a crude tent for shelter. "Too bad we can't always find trees the right distance apart, and where it's flat." Then he spread the second tarp and blankets the way he'd done the night before. "Now let her rip!"

Hastily Josh ate, gave Wolf a portion, and crawled into the tent. There was no sitting around the campfire that night. The long hours in the saddle had left him exhausted. Josh was asleep in five minutes, unaware when the storm broke in full fury.

The bawling of the terrified animals finally woke him. Even above the rain rattling on his tent he could hear the herd. A flash of lightning showed the scene through the open end of his shelter. The cattle milled around on the verge of stampede! Their eyes rolled and they lunged against one another.

"Great!" Josh felt for his boots, climbed into them, and grabbed the slicker he'd made sure was nearby. Wolf was already out of the tent. In the almost-continuous flare of the lightning Josh could see the dog working his way around behind the herd. One extra bright flash showed him nipping at the heels of a wanderer.

Again Josh didn't bother to saddle Ebony. He snatched the hobbles free, slid to her back, and began circling the cattle, working with Wolf. Still the frightened animals continued to bolt. If only Pa were here! What would he do if he were? Josh wondered. Like a voice in his ear came the memory of Pa's comment, "When cattle get milling, sometimes singing to them helps."

Josh howled out a song at the top of his lungs. A few of the closer cattle quieted a little.

He yelled out another, one of the ballads he'd learned when he was small. Although the lightning still flashed, the thunder had moved back into its distant lair. His voice was now stronger than the wind and storm. Gradually the herd stilled, although he could sense they were still restless.

From ballads to hymns Josh progressed, trying to forget his own misery in keeping the herd pacified. Once he grinned between verses. What would old man Sievers think if he could see him now—lullabying a bunch of critters with church songs? He probably *did* look pretty ridiculous out in the middle of a storm hollering:

"Joy to the world, the Lord is come!
Let earth receive her King."

By now he had run out of regular songs. Besides, he always liked Christmas tunes. But as the cattle still milled restlessly and he sang on, even "Away in a Manger" got tiresome.

Josh sang until his voice was hoarse and cracked,

but his herd finally returned to a halfway calm state. The rain let up and the lightning reluctantly moved on, seeking other glades and meadows to brighten. Finally he felt it was safe to leave the cattle and trudge wearily back to his tent. Bedraggled and dirty, Wolf had to be rubbed dry before he could crawl in with him. When had bed felt so good? Josh felt like he could sleep forever. But in this case forever would be only a few hours. He needed to get the herd to water. "As if we didn't have enough here," he drowsily told his faithful dog. The next moment he was asleep.

"Owww!" Josh tried to sit up and fell back on his bed. Wolf leaped straight up, landing on all fours and barking wildly.

Again the boy struggled to sit up. "Every bone in my body feels broken." Cautiously he rolled over, getting to his knees, then boosting himself up. "Will I ever ride again?" He limped to Ebony and unhobbled him. Concern for the drenched horse overrode his own aches. Grabbing an old rag, he wiped the horse down. Ebony whinnied his thanks.

"Well, herd," Josh faced the cattle eyeing him. "It'll be a long day."

It was. The only thing that saved Josh was the fact that the cattle were as tired as he was after their wild night. The passing storm left sunshine behind, and the herd contentedly ambled along the trail in front of Wolf. Josh found himself dozing in the saddle in the warm afternoon sun and finally called a halt. No use trying to go on. Better to get a good rest before tackling the next day's trek.

He didn't put up the tarp—just dropped to the ground even before bothering with supper. All he wanted was sleep. When he came alive again the sun had already set. Wolf lay motionless at his side. Ebony slept standing up. The cattle quietly grazed.

Josh stretched. Funny how just a few hours' sleep could make a new person of him. Starved, he hastily heated water, dropped rice in, and left it to cook. His high spirits had returned. "Hey, Wolf, the first time Charity cooked rice she didn't know how much to fix. She kept adding rice and ended up with about a washtub full. We ate rice pudding, rice with honey, rice with soup, and about a million other rice dishes before it was all gone." He munched on a biscuit while waiting for the hot rice. "Think I'll soak some beans, too. There's never time to do that then get them cooked when we stop. Maybe I can soak them overnight, let them start cooking in the morning, and finish them tomorrow night."

It took Josh and his little group a day and a half to get to good water. Fortunately the storm had left small pools in the low marshy places. While it didn't satisfy the cattle, it did hold them until they reached a better source. Josh knew when the herd smelled water. They'd crossed a mound and headed down toward a shallow ravine. Suddenly the cattle increased their pace. Then again. It was all Josh, Ebony, and Wolf could do to hold them back from full stampede.

"Glad this isn't too steep," Josh panted, heading back still another calf. Anxiously he glanced down the rolling draw. The glint of water through the trees told him they were close.

Shoving and bawling, the herd reached the edge of the water, waded in, and drank thirstily. Josh stared. "Will you look at that!"

What had been a dry wash was a raging flood. Muddy, roiling, the stream spilled over both banks.

Small trees sailed by. A scared-looking rabbit rode one of them.

Ebony edged closer, drank, snorted, and drank again. Josh couldn't tear his eyes from the scene. He'd never seen such a flood. How could all that water come from one storm a few days before?

"So who cares?" he told himself. "What's important is—we have to *cross* that stuff."

It took a long time for the cattle and Ebony to quench their thirst, but Josh patiently waited. He'd found where a clear stream came in, and drank deeply himself. All the while his mind wrestled with a problem. They had to get to the other side, but it was impossible to cross there. Therefore he would have to leave the trail and look for a better place to cross. Studying the land upstream, he shook his head. No, it would be too hard going.

Downstream was better. Although the water filled the bottom of the ravine, it was fairly flat along the edges. "We can't camp in here, though," Josh told his horse. "We'll have to drive them back from the river for the night, then work our way down." With one hand he wiped his sweaty face. "It's going to throw us off schedule, but there's no choice."

Once he had made the decision, he felt better. It was what Pa would do. He turned the reluctant cattle from the muddy stream and started them out to find a camp safe from any possible flash floods pouring more water down the draw.

Quicksand!

Every morning and every night since leaving home, Josh had counted the cattle. ". . . twenty-three, twenty-four, twenty-five," he would finish. It always gave him a good feeling. Pa and Ma would think he was a good steward.

The morning after the dry march he tallied again. ". . . twenty-two, twenty-three, twenty-four—"

A sick feeling hit the pit of his stomach. He counted again. There were still only twenty-four.

He closed his eyes, trying to visualize the herd. Working with it had made each animal distinctive, an individual. Could he remember which was lost or strayed? The howl of the wolf had been closer last night. Could that twenty-fifth critter have been . . . No! "It's just wandered away," Josh told his dog. "But which one is it?" Carefully he studied each animal again. Then he snorted in disgust. "Wouldn't you know it's old Crumple Horn? That ornery steer Charity named after the cow in the poem about the house Jack built. It would be him." Josh sighed. "Well, Wolf, we have to go find him." Quickly he saddled his horse, looked longingly at the now-dead ashes of his fire and wished he had time for breakfast, then shook his head.

"No telling where that beast's gotten to by now."

The rest of the herd lay quietly with no signs of restlessness. "I guess you'll be all right," Josh said. "There's grass and you had a good fill of water last—" he broke off. "Water! I bet that crazy steer headed for the river."

Fear leaped through him. There could be quicksand pools along the flooded river. If Crumple Horn got mired deep, how would they ever get him out?

Josh abandoned any search near camp. He'd check the river first. Ebony was rested and raring to go. It didn't take long to cross the meadow and skim through the cottonwood trees showering the ground with leaves. Long before they reached the river Josh heard a hoarse bawling.

"Crumple Horn! Horse, make tracks." Ebony responded with a leap and a few minutes later they burst through the thicket to the edge of the river. It was exactly what Josh had feared. Crumple Horn was stuck. Muddy water eddied around him. The more the steer struggled, the deeper he sank.

"Don't try and lunge!" Josh screamed but the animal couldn't understand. The pulling, sucking mud terrified him. He fought it again—and sank until only his head and chest remained above the greedy quicksand.

Josh leaped from Ebony's back and ran to the edge of the pool. Crumple Horn bellowed and rolled his great eyes.

"If only you knew what to do," Josh cried through a blur of frustrated tears. "If you'd just stop thrashing around, the mud wouldn't get you so fast." He measured the distance between safe ground and the trapped steer. With unsteady fingers he grabbed his lariat and swung it. If he could lasso the creature's horns, Ebony could drag him from the mire.

Josh swung his right arm. The lariat whistled in a loop above his head. Over, out—it missed.

Wolf ran along the bank frantically barking. Crumple Horn's bellow grew fainter. A horrid ringing assaulted Josh's ears.

"Have to make a longer loop," he muttered. "Fell short about five feet." Trying to shut out the sight and sound of the steer's desperation, he recoiled his lariat. Again it whistled through the air.

"Yippee!" The noose gently settled around the tough horns of the steer's head—all he could see of Crumple Horn. "Whoa, there," Josh shouted. Sweat stood out on his face. He yanked the rope tight, took a turn around the saddle horn, and squeezed Ebony's sides with his knees. "All right, old boy. Back."

The black horse quivered, snorted, then strained backwards.

Nothing happened.

"Come on, Ebony." Josh pulled on the lariat until it was taut. Then he felt as if every muscle in his back was being torn from its place. Slowly Crumple Horn's heaving chest rose from the quicksand.

"Back, boy, back!" Sweat ran down into his eyes. He couldn't spare a hand to wipe it off and his vision blurred.

Ebony stumbled. *The next instant Crumple Horn sank back into the mire.*

"God, help us," the boy screamed. "We can't do it by ourselves!"

Ebony struggled to a steadier position. Inch by inch he fought the slippery bank, backing to safe ground. And inch by inch Crumple Horn slithered and slid, resisting every step of the way.

"You stupid critter, quit fighting us," Josh ordered, but Crumple Horn continued tossing his head, making it even harder to pull him out.

"One more time." Then, "Wolf, do something."

The dog responded with a mighty bark. Crumple Horn bellowed, gave a lurch, and with a sucking sound the mud fell away, leaving one filthy steer at the end of a lariat.

"Thank You, God!" Josh nearly fell from his horse from the wave of relief that surged through him. Tears washed his eyes clean. "Now, number twenty-five, you get back with the rest of the herd and stay there!"

The animal snorted.

"You ungrateful wretch!" Josh loosened the lariat and Wolf headed the steer back toward camp. Several yards downstream Crumple Horn lunged for a pool of water surrounded by willows, wallowed in it, and came forth a few shades lighter.

Suddenly tired, Josh watched the dog head toward the rest of the herd, nipping at Crumple Horn's heels enough to let him know he meant business.

"Ebony, you're all right." Josh slid from the saddle and hugged the horse's wet neck. The heaving horse settled down, whinnied, and nosed Josh, then trotted a few feet and whinnied again.

"All right, all right." The boy swung to the saddle and let the animal take the lead.

It was slow moving for them that day. Josh searched the river banks for a safe place to cross and found none. His original plan had been to ford the river and make camp over the Sabbath. But the water was just too high. Even going miles downstream he found nothing but raging floodwaters. He attempted riding Ebony into the water a few times but gave up. Even if he and the horse made it across, there was no way he could force the cattle to swim it. By late afternoon they were miles out of their way, with no sign in sight of any place to reach the other side.

"We'll make camp here," Josh finally decided. A little clearing seemed ideal; it had lots of browse for the animals and was close enough for Josh to water the animals without traveling far. By the time he had camp set up, supper over, and the chores done, the sun was just kissing the ridge above him goodnight. Moments later Josh wrapped a blanket around him and lay down. Yet, tired as he was, sleep didn't come. He kept remembering the experience with the quicksand. It wasn't until he thought of his prayer, and how he had gradually freed the animal that some of the tightness went out of him.

"Funny," his hand fell to the shaggy head beside him, "I wondered if we'd recognize when God helped us on the trail. All you and Ebony and I could do wasn't enough. But God didn't just yank Crumple Horn free. He just helped us work together." It was a new thought. "Hey, Wolf, s'pose that's the way it always is? God expects us to do what we can, then helps us do more?"

It was too much for a tired brain. Josh slid farther down in his blankets and closed his eyes.

He awoke to blue skies and singing birds. "What a day!" His sleep-filled eyes opened wide. A soft early-morning hush lay on the land. Frost covered everything but was melting a little before the sun. Piles of golden leaves shivered in a slight breeze that brought the mingling of the pungent sage and cedar and high mountain air.

It was the strangest Sabbath Josh remembered.

47

Nothing like at home, where they sang hymns and shared and read the Bible. Even though he did many of the things they always did, it wasn't the same. His voice sounded small in the big land.

Much of the day he lay in his open-ended tent just thinking. Soon he would be a man, not just for a trail drive, but for always. "I want to be the kind of man Pa is," he whispered to Wolf who drowsed beside him. Memories of his father danced in the soft afternoon's light: Pa, riding to help anyone who needed him; Pa, whose gentle hands could heal a hurt or birth an animal; Pa, laughing with baby Mercy bouncing on his knee; Pa, always there, never too tired to see a sunset or walk with his children when chores were done.

Suddenly Josh wanted to tell his father how much he loved him. Of course Pa already knew, but Josh wanted to say it out loud. Wolf stirred. "Guess you're the only one to talk to. Ebony's asleep and who wants to talk to critters?" He fell silent. It was so hard to put into words what he felt somewhere down by his stomach.

"You don't know Pa very well, yet," he told the relaxed dog. "But you will. He's the best pa ever a boy had. You know, the kind that makes folks come up to me and say, 'If you ever be a man like your father you'll be a good one.' When he says something, he does it. Everybody knows that. And he sure does what he thinks is right." His hand stilled and the dog slid closer.

"You know when I asked if we were going to travel on the Sabbath? I already knew what Pa'd say. Even though it might snow and we're in a hurry, he'd say that was no reason not to keep the Sabbath holy. Folks talk all the time about how strict he is towards things of the Lord." Josh's mind raced back.

48

"I remember last summer. A big storm was supposed to be coming down from the mountains. We worked hard but there was still hay in the field.

"'Are we going to finish?' I asked.

"'Not on the Sabbath.' Pa set his lips tight and looked at the sky.

"'But what if the hay gets rained on?' I wanted to know.

"'Keeping the Sabbath is our job, son. Not worrying over the hay.'"

Josh laughed and Wolf sat up and stared at him. "Know what, old boy? Pa was the only settler who wouldn't work on the Sabbath—but his hay *never once got rained on.* All the folks around us couldn't understand it, but that's just what happened." He lay quiet for a long time, then added, "I'm glad Pa's like that."

Wolf didn't answer except to lick Josh's brown hand and snuggle back down.

The boy grinned and lapsed into silence but his mind went on. It really was funny. He'd always worshiped God, had accepted God's Son Jesus as his own personal Saviour when he was just a tad. He'd felt good when his parents told Bible stories and when they sang church songs. And he'd even felt kind of shaky inside when Pa and Ma prayed out loud, or when he prayed at night.

But he'd never felt so close to God as out here along with a dog, a horse, and twenty-five cattle to get to Wyoming. Did God see and love the quaking, golden aspens as much as Josh did? Did He know how cold and good it felt to taste the water in the streams? He must. God made them all.

A sense of God's true greatness filled him. How

could God have created so many things? The birds outside singing praises were perfect. So were the squirrels and rabbits and deer.

"I bet God really had a good time doing all this," Josh whispered so low even Wolf didn't hear him. "I bet He smiled when He put stripes on the chipmunks and skunks and quills on old Quill-Thrower." Josh had never thought much about it before. But out here there was time to do that. A golden-brown head popped up and two black eyes peered at Josh from a few feet away. When the boy didn't move, the tiny chipmunk edged closer. Josh could see its inquisitive nose twitch. Then the boy sneezed. The chipmunk whisked away and into the branches of a nearby tree.

"Thank You, God, for . . ." it was hard to say what he felt. He tried again. "Just, thanks for everything." The sunlit day faded. His weary body relaxed. Secure and content, Josh slept.

Something Lost

It took two days to find a place where the river looked safe enough to cross. Even there the water roiled and beat against the sloping banks.

Josh reined in Ebony. "Shall we try it here?"

The horse snorted and threw back his head, as if he wasn't too enthusiastic about the idea.

The boy sighed. "Wolf, stay with the herd. Ebony, you and I will ride on down the river a ways and see if there's a better place."

There wasn't. Josh rode for several miles through thickets and around high banks. The only crossing was where he'd left the herd. "Maybe we should go back to the regular crossing." He gazed anxiously up the raging river, then at the sky and shook his head. "That's no good. It looks like rain again, and if it does come, the crossing wouldn't be any better than when we were there before." Discouraged, tired, pale from nights of being awakened by the cattle and singing them to sleep, Josh slowly headed back upstream. What had been an adventure had turned into a grinding, tough job. More than once he'd considered turning back, but wouldn't give up. The herd *had* to get to Wyoming and there was no one to take it there except him.

51

When he got back to Wolf and his charges, the boy took time to consider what he should do. Should he separate part of the herd and make more than one trip? Or would the cattle be better off swimming together? Wouldn't the calves be terrified if they couldn't see their mothers?

"I guess it's all or nothing." Josh wiped his sweaty face with a dirty hand. He took a deep breath, patted Ebony, and called Wolf. Carefully he eased the herd into one bunch, rode Ebony to a position that would be behind and downstream of them, then gave a mighty yell. "Hi, yi, get moving, cattle!"

Crumple Horn took the lead. Josh smacked his open hand against the leather of his saddle. "Get going, Crumple Horn!" He sent Ebony forward and urged the steer into the water.

The animal lurched forward, then hesitated. Was he remembering the quicksand?

"After him, Wolf!"

The dog bounded toward Crumple Horn, barking furiously. Josh yelled again. Evidently the terrors ahead weren't as scary as the awful noise behind him. Crumple Horn plunged into the swollen river and began to swim, angling a little downstream.

"Good, the current will put you out on that partly covered sandbar." Josh watched until the big steer stumbled from the water onto dry ground, then turned back to the rest of the herd. A few had followed Crumple Horn. Others held back. Their bawling echoed across the quiet land.

"Get in that river, you!" Josh drove, prodded, and pushed the cattle. Some balked, refusing to go. Wolf handled those. He seemed to know just when and where he could do the most good. Time after time he nipped at the heels of the very animal that was most reluctant.

It seemed like hours later but was probably only a few minutes that the entire herd was in the water, thrashing and milling and bellowing. Even the calves were all right, held in by the press of the other cattle and swimming with the current.

"Oh, oh!" a wave caught one of the calves off balance and it lost its footing. In a flash Ebony was after it, automatically swimming out and around so the calf was upstream. Josh saw the calf regain control at the same time he spotted a new danger—a large tree branch rushing toward them.

"Watch out, boy!"

His warning came too late. The branch missed the still-swimming calf, but raked Ebony with a long limb as it passed, just enough to make his mount stumble.

A wall of water hit the horse, and the saddle shifted beneath the boy. Ebony's head disappeared under the muddy water. Josh hung on, his hands clutching the reins, legs gripping Ebony like a vise.

The black horse struggled against the current. Silently praying without words ever leaving his parched throat, Josh clung to the horse. They were swept around a bend. The boy could no longer see the cattle herd, but he could hear Wolf howling. Would the dog get the stragglers safely across?

Every second Josh expected Ebony to go down, but the horse fought to remain on the surface. Gradually Ebony gained control of the situation. The current still slowed him but they were nearer the opposite shore. Weak and spent, the horse at last reached shallower water, blew out a great breath, and climbed the low bank to dry land.

Josh's numb fingers slipped from the reins and he fell from the saddle, sliding to the ground. Ebony's knees buckled and he collapsed beside the panting, white-faced boy.

As he lay half senseless, Josh could hardly believe they were still alive. The angry river swept on, looking for new victims, but Josh didn't hear it. The roaring in his ears was not just from the river. He spit out river water that had filled his mouth, hating its taste, hating the river that had nearly claimed him. Closing his eyes, he could picture what could have been—Ebony and him sinking to the bottom.

Suddenly he sprang to his feet, freckles dark on his streaked face. "No, we're alive! Ebony—" his voice broke. Had there ever been a horse to match him? What a comrade!

A wild cry escaped Josh's lips. "Our Third Comrade saved us, Ebony." Some of the rolling in Josh's stomach settled. "Even when I couldn't say a prayer out loud, He heard." Thankfulness filled him. "God, I . . ." he couldn't go on. Somehow he didn't think it mattered.

A distant howl roused the boy again. "Wolf! We have to go see about the herd." Wearily and stiffly he walked to Ebony. "Are you all right, old boy?"

Ebony scrambled to his feet, pawed the air with one foot, then the other as if checking to see that he was whole. Still panting, he nuzzled Josh. Except for a long scratch on one shoulder he seemed fine.

"You get an extra measure of oats tonight." Then dismay flooded through him. "The saddlebags! They're gone!" Frantically he looked downstream. "When did they come loose?" He ran a few steps along the bank. "All our food. The Bible. Everything except bedroll and tarp. God, *what are we going to do?*"

Only the rush of the river answered. Josh stared at it, fierce tears burning his cheeks. They couldn't go back—they could never cross that river again. There was nothing ahead but wilderness. It was too late in the year for berries. Could he live on just water? Why couldn't he have been fat instead of skinny? How long could a skinny kid get by with nothing to eat—and they were days late because of the flood.

"We have to check the cattle first," he told his exhausted horse. "Then I'll take you and see if the saddlebags might have been washed up on the shore anywhere."

Dragging and tired, the two headed back toward the herd. They had been swept a good quarter mile or more down the river. "I hope we didn't lose any stock," Josh said. "If only Wolf . . ." The idea died on his lips. Wolf was a great dog, but herding twenty-five head of cattle across a treacherous river was a lot to ask.

When he reached the herd they were lying down on the riverbank, above the stream and danger. Wolf stood guard.

A rush of love for the dog swept through him. "You did it, boy! Did you save them all? I'd never have seen if some were swept away. We were too busy trying to get out of the river." Hope mingled with fear as he began his tally. "One . . . two . . . three . . ." He counted slowly, making sure he missed none of them. "Twenty-two . . . twenty-three . . . twenty-four—" His heart sank. One was gone.

It was the last straw. Slumping to the ground, he began to sob. Why had he ever told Pa he could handle this man-size job when he wasn't a man—just a weak, miserable kid with big ideas?

The brush rustled. Stilled. Rustled again.

Great! What now, some new danger?

Josh held his breath. Another rustle, then the brush parted. A head thrust through. "Moooo . . ."

"Hooray!" Number twenty-five was safe and all was well, at least with the cattle.

"Sorry to do this to you, Ebony," Josh apologized. "But we have to go see if we can find those saddlebags before dark." Stiffly he climbed aboard the tired horse.

It was slow going. This side of the river was rougher than the other. Several times the boy had to leave Ebony on a high bank and crawl down nearer the water when he saw something that might be the saddlebags. Because the gray day made everything look mysteriously changed, Josh almost missed what he was searching for.

"God—is that it?" He scrambled to a partly submerged tree at the edge of the water. One long branch went out into the water. The boy lay full length and slid along on his belly. "It is!" He snatched the saddlebags. The sudden movement tilted the branch and ducked his head under water. The branch shifted, and as he came up sputtering but still clutching his prize, he heard a frightening *crack*. Carefully he backed his way off the now-broken branch and got back to shore, noticing how far through the narrow perch had broken under his weight.

"We've got it!" he triumphantly told Ebony. Eagerly he opened the saddlebags, then groaned. Water poured from the bags. From the flour sack. The rice. The beans. The salt. Even the Bible, wrapped in an oiled piece of cloth, had wet edges. Ebony's oats were a soggy mass.

Josh stared, beaten. Hadn't God heard his prayer? "Hold it," he ordered himself. "God's taken care of us so far. We're better off than we were in the water. Or before we found the saddlebags. I'll cook everything up and carry it cooked. As long as the matches are dry I'm all right." He felt the carefully wrapped package in his shirt, buttoned and pinned for safety. "Come on, horse, let's get back to the cattle."

Josh spent all evening cooking the rest of his meager supplies. Much of the flour was ruined beyond use. He made hard biscuits with the rest, heating his Dutch oven in a bed of coals, warming the cover, and putting the biscuits inside, then covering the top with coals, too. They weren't the greatest in the world, but they'd do. Next he tried cooking the oats to see whether Ebony would eat them, but the big horse didn't like them. Josh thoughtfully tried them himself. They weren't too good, but he couldn't afford to waste anything that might serve as food. If his sugar hadn't been ruined they'd have been OK.

It was cold and clear again after a day of misty driving rain. Josh's spirits rose. Things weren't all bad, though he'd have to skimp on meals. It would take several days to get back to the trail. Would it be possible to try a short-cut and and make up the time they'd lost? Every time the fog lifted he could see snow lower on the peaks ahead.

"Better not," Josh decided. "If we got out there somewhere and got lost, no one would even know where to look for us." Carefully he packed his supplies. "Good thing the Dutch oven and tin plate were wrapped in my bedroll." He fastened it behind the saddle and stowed his food back in the saddlebags, making sure they were tight. "I hope there are no more floods to cross but we'll be sure and be prepared."

Like an arrow from a bow came Pa's words, "He's

prepared as far as food, a map, and determination. Now we need to make sure he's really prepared . . ." A longing for his father's wisdom and steady, guiding hand welled up inside the boy. Gently he opened the big Bible. Some of the pages were stained, although he'd tried to dry them last night. He flipped to a marker Pa'd put in.

"Listen to this, Wolf. 'God is our refuge and strength, a very present help in trouble. Therefore will not we fear . . . ; though the waters thereof roar and be troubled . . .' It's from the forty-sixth psalm." He closed the Bible and tucked it in the saddlebag.

"Well, God's been with us in the quicksand and the waters—now for the trail back to where we should have been almost a week ago." Noticing how the trees had grown bare in the few days they'd been on the drive, he shivered. Only a few golden leaves clung to the aspens. They looked lonely and cold, like an old woman who'd lost her coat in winter.

"Standing here dreaming won't get us on our way," Josh announced. "Come on, critters, let's get going again."

Long Way
to Wyoming

The trail back to the river crossing was long and hard. Sometimes Josh and his little band had to leave the river and double back to get around long stretches of high bank and streams rushing in. Every time they forded even runoff water left over from the flash flood something curled inside Josh. The steady rain didn't help. He couldn't seem to stay dry. Even his slicker only kept him dry to about the knees. His feet and legs took the worst of it. At night he rubbed them when they were so numb from the cold rain and mud that they ached.

One particularly soggy afternoon his stomach growled especially loud in protest. No matter how much he knew he had to save what food he had, his stomach wouldn't accept it. The hollowness inside felt like the inside of a big dark cave Pa had once shown him. Even after he got back on the better-traveled trail every foot of the way seemed longer.

The second Sabbath was nothing like the first. Josh found what shelter he could, put up his tarp, and spent the day in his blankets. He tried to read the Bible but his complaining stomach bothered him and he couldn't concentrate. His prayers had come down to a simple,

"Lord, take care of us and get us all through safely."

The next day the clouds drifted ahead of a cold wind. Streaks of sunshine cast pale rays on the trail. "I always feel better when the sun shines," he told Wolf.

The dog licked his lips hungrily. He'd had to go on short rations, too. Ebony and the herd fared better since there was plenty of browse.

"They're getting fatter and we're getting skinnier," Josh laughed. It sounded loud in the morning air. A crow flying by answered with a raucous screech while a chattering squirrel scolded from a low branch nearby. Wolf made a futile dash toward it, but the squirrel was too fast and disappeared, then stuck its head out farther up the tree and scolded again.

By afternoon Josh could see water ahead, lots of it.

"Anyway, we're on the right trail," he rejoiced. "You know, dog, that trail got so dim back there from no one using it I was beginning to wonder if we'd strayed. We haven't. That's Bear Lake. We're about halfway there—but what a long time it's taken!"

The herd broke from a plodding walk into a quicker pace. Did the sight of the sparkling lake encourage them? "Get along, critters," Josh prodded. They needed no urging. A little later they trotted down a slope and to the lake.

Josh unsaddled Ebony and watched him follow the cattle. First he drank, then wallowed in the water near the edge of the lake.

"Me too," Josh said to Wolf. "Baths for both of us, old boy. But first we make camp."

The novelty of choosing trees for his rope and hanging the tarp, making his bed, arranging stones for a fireplace, and all the other camp chores had long since worn off. Now slow hands performed the tasks.

When he was done he took stock of his supplies. Rebellion filled him. Would it be any worse to be hungry the last few days than to be half starved now?

"I'll do it," he muttered. "I'll eat as much as I can hold tonight. Today I almost fell from the saddle from being so hungry. It shouldn't take more than five extra days to get to Wyoming. There are half a dozen biscuits left and some rice. A little of the cooked oats, too." He grimaced. The oats were terrible. Every time he reheated them they tasted worse.

Josh intended to save a biscuit a day for the trail. But when he ate the rest of the food he couldn't stop. He was so hungry he stuffed in biscuit after biscuit. "Besides," he glared at Wolf who watched with accusing eyes until Josh tossed the last two over to him, "the biscuits were getting moldy on one side. Better to eat them than to waste them."

Almost instantly he knew he'd made a bad mistake. Not only had he consumed the rest of his stores, his shriveled stomach couldn't handle the soggy food in its present condition. Tears streaming down his face, he lurched to the bushes, his stomach tied in knots.

When it was all over he lay on his blankets, worn out. "Serves me right," he said brokenly. "I shoulda known better."

But what was he to do now? He was worse off than he'd been before. Five days without food lay ahead. Five days to Wyoming. The Salt River pass. Snow in the offing. Restless cattle.

"Well, God, here I am again. If ever I needed You, it's now." He fell asleep clutching his shrunken, queasy stomach.

It was daylight when he woke. At least the sun had struggled up. Josh felt his forehead, wondering why it was so warm. Oh, yeah, he'd been half sick last night. He scrabbled in his saddlebag for crumbs, hoping against hope he'd missed a biscuit or something but he hadn't.

The lake lay smooth and still. Josh looked at his filthy hands. The floodwaters had been so muddy he hadn't been able to have a bath. The lake was bound to be icy but at least he'd be clean.

With Wolf bounding after him, Josh carefully tested the water's depth from the slight bank above it. He wasn't much of a swimmer, and he wasn't about to get in over his head. Several hundred yards from where his cattle lay he found a shallow beach. There he could get in and out easily.

Josh started to unbutton his shirt then stopped. "It's even dirtier than I am, Wolf. So are my jeans. I'll just take my boots off and get the matches out of my pocket so they're safe, then go in with my clothes on. That way they'll get a little washed and I'll crawl into my other outfit." Racing back to camp, he grabbed a pair of patched jeans, a shirt, and wool socks. Returning to where Wolf stood, he coaxed him, "In, boy, in."

The dog didn't budge.

"Come on, Wolf, you're one dirty animal." Josh stepped into the lake. "Oww! Is this ever cold!" His teeth chattered but he forced himself to duck under, only to shoot to the surface like a bullet from a rifle. He'd never known colder water in his whole life. Gasping, he charged back to land. "No w-wonder you w-wouldn't c-come in." He snatched the big rough towel Ma had hemstitched, stripped the wet clothes off, and rubbed his body dry. Did the clean clothes ever feel good! Wiping his face, he scrubbed the towel across his wet hair, then pulled on a cap. The mid-October sun hadn't lived up to its false promise of warmth. It wasn't until he shrugged into his heavy jacket and built up his fire that he stopped shaking.

"I can at least have something hot to drink." Josh rummaged in his all but empty pack. He'd managed to salvage a bit of the herbal tea leaves his father had given him. They had somehow escaped the water when he lost the saddlebags—maybe because they were so well wrapped.

The hot brew revived him, but his stomach continued to protest. He needed food, not just a drink.

"Be still, stomach. If we don't have any food, we don't have any food. That's all there is to it." He clasped both hands tightly across his shrunken waistline. A squirrel ran by, busy on some business of his own.

"Hey!" Josh sat up straight. "Maybe I can find where he stores nuts for the winter. Or acorns, or something. Can a person boil acorns?" Silently he crossed the clearing, eyes fixed on the squirrel. A slithering behind him brought his eyes back. "Stay, Wolf!" He crept on but had lost track of the squirrel.

"Great!" He sighed. "Well, better hit the trail. We might as well be hungry in Idaho as in Utah. We'll probably make it into the corner tonight."

A stick cracked. That couldn't be Wolf. He heard a horse neigh. "Ebony?" But the horse was standing stock-still where he'd left him. Icy fingers wiggled up Josh's back as he looked back across the clearing.

Four men on horseback were in his camp.

"Hey, Bill," one yelled. "There's a bunch of cattle over here."

"Wonder where their owner is." The one called Bill glanced around the camp with glittering dark eyes.

"Funny—doesn't seem like anyone should be out here this time of year."

"Here's a tent. An' a Bible. Ain't that pecooliar?"

Josh dove to the ground and lay still. Who on earth were these men? Pa had said it wasn't likely there'd be anyone on the trail. Were they rustlers? Every frontier tale Josh had ever heard rose in his mind. He scanned the outfit. Rough clothes, strong horses, rifles in holsters, bedrolls, and saddlebags. Whoever they were, they'd been out a while. Their boots were as muddy as his had been before he cleaned them. Sweat stains showed around the bands of their hats.

"Anyone here?" boomed a crude voice.

He couldn't stay here hiding, no matter who they turned out to be. First of all, they'd be bound to find him. Next, Ebony and the cattle were his responsibility. God wouldn't let him come all this way then get held up by rustlers, would He?

Wolf growled.

One of the men drew his rifle. "There's a wolf! How come he's out in broad daylight?"

Josh heard the click as the rider threw a shell into the rifle chamber. "Hold it! He's not a wolf. He's a dog." The boy ran across the short space separating them with Wolf right behind him, still growling. "Quiet, Wolf!"

"Well, can you beat that!" The cowboy dropped his rifle and stared. "Wolf? Reckon I wasn't so far off at that.

"What you doin' out here, sonny?" The man's dark eyes weren't so threatening up close. He looked kind. His furrowed face lit with a smile. "You ain't alone with these cattle, are you?"

Josh nodded. "I'm taking them to Wyoming for my Pa."

The men exchanged glances. Some of the fear drained from the boy. They didn't act like rustlers and were pretty friendly, really.

"How come your Pa let you come alone this time of year?" The spokesman's face turned red with disapproval.

"We'd sold our place. Old man Sievers would never have let us stay longer, even after Pa got hurt . . ." Quickly he related the whole story.

" 'Pears you've been on the trail a lot longer than necessary," a keen-eyed man put in. "Where's your supplies?"

"Gone. Wolf and I ate the last of the biscuits yesterday."

"Whew! An' you with a bunch of miles ahead?" The leader ran a calloused hand over his grizzled chin.

"It isn't our fault. We got caught in the flood." Josh explained what had happened.

"Well, now, I reckon four hunters just might be able to spare enough grub to get one plucky kid down the trail, huh, men?"

"Hunters!" Relief weakened Josh's knees.

"Shore. What'd you take us for, rustlers?" The men didn't wait for an answer. "Haw, haw! That's a good one on us."

"How old're you, kid?" The man who thought the boy's dog was really a wolf wanted to know.

"Thirteen soon. My birthday's the twentieth."

"You should just about make it." The hunter glanced at the mountains and sky then said, "If you want to stick with us 'til we're through with our hunt, we could ride with you far as the pass."

The offer left Josh torn with indecision. Should he wait? It would give him company and help. But he'd have to pull the cattle off the trail and Pa would be heading for Wyoming soon. When he didn't find his son and reached their new home, he'd be worried sick. Ma and Charity'd worry even more. "Thanks, but I better keep moving."

"Not a bad idee at that. Trail's open now, an' it might not be when we leave." The hunter cocked his head and listened to one of the steers bellowing from the herd. "You wouldn't want to sell us one of those critters, would you? Fresh meat'd taste good an' we ain't had no luck huntin' yet."

Josh shook his head again. His hair fell into his eyes and he shoved it back. "Naw. Pa sent twenty-five head of cattle and I have to get twenty-five to Wyoming."

"It's a long way to Wyomin', but I know how you feel. I'll not be interfering with what your pa told you to do. Here, you Tom, get a sack of stuff made up for the kid. Bill Mitchell's never turned nobody away hungry and this kid could stand some fattening up." He turned back to Josh. "You said ol' man Sievers?"

"Yes." Josh could barely tear his eyes from the bread and cheese and dried fruit Tom stuffed in the saddlebags. As soon as he got out of sight he'd eat, but this time he'd know when to quit.

"Thought so. I've heard of the ol' skinflint." Bill held out his hand and gripped the boy's. "Good luck on the trail, kid—what'd you say your name was?"

"Josh Kincaid."

Bill swung to the saddle, followed by his men. "Well, Josh Kincaid, you tell your pa he's got a mighty fine kid. If you need a job in a few years punching cows you look me up down Evanston way." He waved aside the boy's thanks and the four headed out.

But just before they disappeared through the trees

Josh heard Bill say, "Can you beat that? Twelve years old and out here driving cattle to Wyomin'! Some kid."

Stranger in Camp

Well, old boy, looks like God did it again." Hurriedly Josh broke camp, stuffing bread and cheese in his mouth while he worked. New strength poured through him. "We're going to make it this time." He cocked his head to the right and stared at the sky. "Hope the weather doesn't change."

Snow lay far down on the ridges now. In a few days Josh and the cattle would be in it if it stayed cloudy. Rain here in the valley was bound to be snow higher up.

The boy sighed. "Just one thing after another. At least, we've got food to get us there." He clambered onto Ebony and started the cattle. They bellowed in protest. "Dumb critters. They're satisfied right here 'cause there's food and water. Oh well, they'll like Wyoming once we get there."

Although the distant peaks glistened and the sky threatened bad weather, the sun stayed out for most of the next couple of days. Josh made good time. Something inside him told him he'd better hurry. It was mid-October and anything could happen if winter came early. He woke up when it was still dark, hastily ate, routed out the cattle, and got moving. Then he traveled until it was too dark to see the trail well and fell into bed with his clothes on. No more time for baths, even if there had been other lakes.

Then one afternoon as he drowsed in the saddle and followed the herd, a moaning sound in the wind brought him wide awake. "Uh-oh. Doesn't sound good, does it, Ebony?" The black horse snorted, listened, snorted again. Wolf circled the herd endlessly. The wind grew stronger, bringing rain, then a chill. Tiny ice pellets mingled with the rain. Soon they slashed against his skin, leaving his exposed face numb.

"We've got to hole up," Josh said. He searched the darkening landscape for shelter and spotted a semi-protected valley ahead, just a little hollow surrounded by rolling ground. Huge evergreens grew close together and would offer some shelter. Expertly Josh drove the herd in close to a huge, overhanging rock. It was big enough to lead Ebony under and still have space for a fire and his bed. "Come on, Wolf."

The big dog hesitated, facing the wind. The hair on his back bristled.

"What's wrong, Wolf?" Josh walked over to where the animal still stood motionless, nose pointed into the growing storm.

Then with a growl he took one padded step forward.

Josh peered into the rapidly increasing darkness. He could see nothing. Still, Wolf's actions bothered him. Did he smell danger? Wild animals would move down from the hills before a storm. Was there something out in the darkness watching them, waiting for . . . what?

Slowly Wolf's hair settled back and he lost the listening, waiting look. Turning, he trotted back to

Ebony and lay down beneath the shelving rock. Whatever had disturbed him must be gone.

Josh wasn't so easily satisfied. If animals did come, he had only the light rifle. What would Pa do? He'd asked himself that a hundred times. Pa had said a steward knew the master so well he acted just like his master would act. Well, Pa expected him to do as a steward would and figure out the answer.

"I know!" the boy cried. "Pa would build a big fire and keep it all night. Wild animals are scared of fire. We'll have to stay awake and feed it." A glance around him revealed plenty of wood. Old lightning-struck snags would be dry in the center. Fallen limbs back under the thick interlaced branches of the evergreens would be dry, too. Josh left his bed-making and supper-getting until later. Now it was his job to drag in as much wood as he could before it got pitch black. The little sleet pellets had changed into soft white flakes before he finished.

Later he looked at the big pile of wood with satisfaction. *"Now* we can eat!" It didn't take long for his simple supper preparations and when he was through he nibbled on a stale cookie Tom had thrown in with the other supplies. "Sure wish Charity could be here." His free hand stroked Wolf's head. "I can just see how those red curls of hers would bounce if she got scared. Her eyes would be bigger than Ma's best platter." As loneliness swept through him he heaved a great sigh. "Well, at least I've got you, dog. And Ebony." He was quiet a long time. His nest under the big rock was cozy and the fire in front made him feel safe. "Best of all, we've got God."

Several times during the night he woke and fed the fire. The snow dwindled off and just before daylight stopped. Josh would have no trouble rounding up the herd. They'd stayed close during the night. But something was definitely wrong with Wolf. He'd prowled and squirmed until Josh had trouble getting enough sleep.

"What's wrong with you?" he asked crossly. "Don't you know in about an hour we have to be on the move?"

The dog didn't even glance at him, but just slunk away with his tail between his legs.

Regret filled the boy. "Sorry, Wolf. You've a right to be restless." He closed his eyes again and yawned but Wolf didn't come back to bed. When he reopened his eyes it was murky but light. Another dark day, maybe with snow.

"Wolf?" Josh struggled into his boots. No answer. "Come on, boy. It's breakfast time." Where was the joyful bark and the slobbery kiss the dog usually gave him?

A little alarmed, Josh walked around the camp. Because about an inch of snow covered the ground, Wolf's tracks were plain, leading away from the rock shelter. The boy followed them. Suddenly he stopped and bent down. "What on earth!" He swallowed hard.

Hand-sized tracks were printed deep in the white snow, just where the circle of firelight would have ended. *And dog tracks led right into them!*

"Bear, and a big one!" Josh felt his freckles pop out. "Wolf, you didn't get in a fight, did you?" Carefully he searched the area for signs of struggle. "I'd have heard if you attacked a bear. Or if one got after you." He stuck his fingers in the tracks. "Nope. You trailed the bear." Holding his breath, Josh carefully moved ahead, eyes glued to the ground. About a quarter mile from camp a curious thing showed in the bear-and-dog trail. The bear tracks veered west. Wolf's tracks headed east. Why?

There didn't seem to be an answer, but he took off after the dog. A little farther on he found what he was looking for. "Oh, no!" The prints told the story. "So it wasn't just the wind. I really did hear a wolf howl last night." Tears of disappointment poured down his cold face. Angrily he brushed them away. "You're a deserter, Wolf! First she-wolf you see, you leave us all out here and take off after her. Well, go, then! Who cares? We'll get to Wyoming without you." Picking up a snow-covered rock, he hurled it east.

It didn't help. Josh felt emptier inside than when he had to go without food. The dog had been his comrade and now he was gone. Even a quick glance showed the smaller wolf tracks that could only have been made by a female.

As he trudged back to camp he couldn't help remembering how he'd yelled at Wolf for bothering him. The dog must have been fighting natural instinct even then. Why hadn't the cattle sensed danger? "We were upwind of the animals," Josh muttered. "The cattle wouldn't have smelled the bear, and the wolf was far enough away so they wouldn't get loco."

Maybe it was his fault Wolf had deserted. Now he just had two comrades for the rest of the trail. He knew dogs could have their feelings hurt. Why did he have to yell like that? Disgust with himself and with Wolf blinded him to the sun that turned the world to sparkles. Some steward he was, not even appreciating his fellow travelers!

It was another long, hard day. By night they were

close to the pass over the Salt River range of mountains. Once across and down, it couldn't be more than about twenty-five miles more. Part of Josh was glad, but another part lingered back by the shelving rock and the telltale tracks in the snow.

Josh's rough day turned into an even worse night. Wood wasn't so easy to find and much of it was green or wet. It took a long time to locate enough to get even a smoldering fire going and keep it burning. Josh was exhausted by the time he ate, and tonight he didn't have Wolf to rouse him when the fire burned low. When he did waken, it was blacker than the inside of a pocket and the fire was nearly out. It took time to get it going again, and by then the boy was wide awake.

Uneasiness hung over him. Usually he slept through those dark, discouraging hours with Wolf beside him. Now he lay sleepless. He could see out the end of his tarp-tent to the fire and a few feet beyond, he could hear the soft movement of the cattle and smell wood smoke. Now and then one of the cattle bawled and Josh's blood turned to ice. If something attacked the herd, could he drive it away? He hadn't known how terrible it would be without Wolf. When he did sleep it was fitfully. His hand automatically reached out for a furry back that wasn't there.

The boy woke more tired than when he'd gone to bed. "The pass for us today." The prospect offered little joy, though. Another threatening sky filled him with gloom. There was bound to be snow. Though unable to put it in words, his heart cried out, "God, somehow this feels like the big test. Please . . ." He couldn't finish. His heart told him God would never leave him the way Wolf had done, but his exhausted brain couldn't acknowledge it. Life had become one long, endless trail, pushing cattle, worrying, and watching the sky.

"Bears and cougars [mountain lions] don't usually attack humans," he told himself. "If there's any real danger it's to the calves. I have to watch them. A calf would be just what a big old bear would like before he goes into hibernation for the winter." His pessimism overcame his usually cheerful attitude. It was hard to be in a good mood when his dog had turned back to wolf and the trail was getting harder and harder.

More and more Josh sank into gloom until he realized what he was doing. "Getting cabin fever, I guess," he told Ebony. "I can see how those old prospectors who had to be penned in all winter went loco by spring." Saying it out loud he felt better. It still spit snow and they could make progress only slowly. Yet something inside him told him things would get better. Maybe God was causing the funny feeling. Whatever it was, Josh started whistling. Ebony pricked up his ears. Even the herd stopped their bawling and went on like they were supposed to.

"I bet they haven't got used to the idea yet that Wolf isn't right behind them," Josh chuckled to himself. A pang went through him. Why couldn't Wolf have stayed true? He was three-quarters dog. How come that one-quarter wolf strain came out? "Maybe it's the same as good parents having kids that act bad. Everybody gets to choose."

All day Josh managed to hang on to his better spirit, but darkness and gloom set in at the same time. One moment it had been light. The next it was practically black. Shelter was poor. No welcome, overhanging rock ledge for protection. Just trees, trees, and more trees. At least there was good water. The boy had found a stream running off the mountain. Its water hurt his teeth it was so cold. "Could be even colder in the morning," he said through chattering teeth. "Reckon I'll take a panful to camp and save having to pack it in the morning."

He stumbled on his way to the stream. A fallen log lay across the trail, and he'd forgotten it was there. The pan went flying, clanging against the log and rolling to one side. A low, ominous sound grew into a roar. Josh froze. The roar came again. It sounded close—too close.

On hands and knees, Josh raised himself from the trail and looked over the top of his frail protection. A few feet away the brush rattled.

"You won't trick me this time, critter!" Josh let out his breath, remembering the porcupine that had scared him before. He started to get up, but was knocked flat.

A bundle of charging fur raced past him, straight at the brush. When the boy managed to get off his back and up, he exclaimed, "Wolf, you're back!"

His joy died immediately. Snarls worse than those the day Mr. Sievers beat Wolf came from the maddened dog. His ears lay almost flat as he crouched ready to spring.

"Wh-what . . . ?" Josh never got the rest of his question out. The bushes parted and a huge, dark shape appeared. It reared up on great hind legs and walked like a giant man. Even the pale campfire light couldn't hide the terrible sight—a hungry, enraged bear heading straight for Wolf and Josh, who had stumbled into his territory.

Ornery Critters

Wolf!" Josh's sharp command came out as a weak whisper. He tried again, but the dog paid no attention as he stood on guard, a frail barrier between the boy and the bear. His barking shattered the night, mingled with the growls of the attacking animal.

"Don't just stand there, stupid; do something!" a voice inside Josh ordered. Tearing his gaze free from the sight, he cautiously stepped backwards and tried to think. Before he could get the rifle and load it the bear might kill Wolf. Besides, he might only wound the bear and then things would be worse. The dog crouched even lower, ready to defend Josh even if it meant death.

"God, what now?" The prayer came out in a sob. His foot hit something that rang. The pan. Could he drive the bear away armed with a solitary pan and prayer? Somehow he had to try. He couldn't just stand there and watch Wolf be chewed to pieces or smashed against a tree from a mighty blow of the bear's paw.

A sense of strength greater than his own shot through him. Grabbing a stout limb from the ground where it had fallen, he beat it on his pan. *"Run, bear! Get out of here!"*

The clanging stopped the beast in his tracks. For an instant he wavered, then dropped to all fours. Josh knew he'd either charge or turn tail. Josh slammed the limb on the pan, beating so hard he could feel dents in the frying pan. At the same time he screamed at the top of his lungs. The bellowing of the now-terrified cattle added to the din. It was too much for the bear. With a final roar he swung around and ran. The dog leaped after him.

"No, Wolf, no!" Tossing the pan aside, he flung himself on the dog. "Let him go! He'd kill you. He's gone now. We're safe."

Gradually Wolf stopped struggling. A big rough tongue licked Josh's hot face. Josh rolled over and over with his dog, laughing and crying and thanking God.

When they finally sat up, the forest was silent except for distant crashings. The bear was gone.

The unnatural stillness struck him square between his eyes. Yes, the bear was gone, but *so was the herd.* He could hear faint bawling in the distance, then it faded and all was still.

"Ebony?" Josh raced back to camp, Wolf beside him. "Hey, horse, are you here?" His mind outdistanced his feet. He'd been so busy with camp chores he'd forgotten to hobble the horse. The boy ran to the tree where he'd left the animal.

Snow was beginning to stick on the branches. Josh peered underneath. The big branches had offered some protection, enough for the tired, drooping horse to lie down or even stand with head hanging. But the space was empty.

At first Josh couldn't believe it. When he stopped searching he sank to the ground, the dog stretched out next to him. "Well, old boy . . ." His voice failed. Cattle gone. Horse gone. Now what?

"It's just you and me and God now," he whispered. "We can't even look for the herd and Ebony until morning."

Wolf pricked up his ears and grumbled but the boy stared unseeing into the fire. "God, this is Your big chance." He couldn't go on—he and his dog were completely at the mercy of the storm. Everything now was up to God.

Strangely enough the thought calmed him. Huddled close to Wolf, he slept dreamlessly, too worn out to worry about anything. Not even the knowledge he couldn't look for the cattle without a horse, or fear of what the next day might bring, could keep him awake.

Josh awoke to three inches of snow covering his tarp and a blue, blue sky smiling at him. "Brr!" He made short work of dressing, fed Wolf, and ate a fast breakfast. Then he knelt down by the big tree. "Well, God, I'm all ready to go hunt the herd. Pa always reads stories from the Bible where You helped people. I guess I need help about as bad as any of them ever did. I can track the cattle—no, I can't either. The snow came afterward. Anyway," he gulped, "I'd sure appreciate it if . . ." If what? If God brought the cattle back? If God rounded up a horse that bolted because he forgot to hobble him?

Shame and regret stopped his prayer. How could he ask God to take over after he'd been so careless?

"I bet that lost sheep didn't get lost because Jesus forgot to put the gate up on the pen," Josh cried. "Pa, I don't know what you'd do right now." Tears blinded him. "I've been a poor steward and now I'm in an awful fix."

For a long time he knelt there, not exactly praying,

just thinking. Pa always said no one deserved the things God gave them. They were free gifts, and Jesus was the best. If God loved Josh enough to send His own Son to die and take the boy's place, then He could help him now.

"I'll just wait, Wolf." Josh stood up, his face set. "But in the meantime, it won't hurt to kind of look around."

They started out from camp into a sugar-frosting world. "Looks like Ma's best white blanket," Josh said. The sun on the snow was so bright it made it hard to see anything. Then Josh saw it—a black blob against the dazzling snow.

He stopped in his tracks, shaded his eyes against the sun. But he still couldn't quite make it out. Was it a big rock? Ebony? The bear? Should he call? Before he got his mouth open, the shape moved. Wolf took off like a shot.

Josh yelled. The next instant Wolf's wild barking smashed the white silence, and a shrill neighing followed.

"Ebony!" His heart leaping, Josh plowed through the snow. The big black horse trotted toward him, then stood with reins dangling.

"So you came back, did you?" Josh buried his face in Ebony's neck, the long mane tickling him. His eyes smarted. "God, You must have sent Ebony. Now, could You help us find the herd, please?"

Locating the herd was easier said than done. The frightened cattle had bellowed their way into safety from the bear and noise. Before Josh spotted even the first of the cattle, the sky had turned dark and daylight began to fade.

Time after time Josh expected to find the animals bunched together. Instead he found them in twos and threes, scattered over a good mile of mountainside. The "ornery critters" as he called them, had been spooked badly. Now they were still nervous and hard to drive. If it hadn't been for Ebony and Wolf, the task would have been almost impossible. Even with their careful herding it was difficult. The snow made for slow going. It did help Josh in one way though—the cattle had moved some after it snowed and left tracks.

"Twenty-two . . . twenty-three . . . twenty-four . . . *twenty-five!*" Josh threw his cap in the air. He wanted to shout, but knew better—he did not want to frighten them away again. "You'd have been easier to find if you'd been sheep or lost lambs, but at least we're all together!" For the first time he glanced around, noticing how dark it had grown. He'd been squinting for a time but it really hadn't registered before.

"Great. Here we are off the trail again." Anxiously he scanned the landscape. The wind that moaned in the trees chilled him. "No, you don't," he told the wind. "Just quit trying to scare me. God's taken care of us this far. Tomorrow we cross the pass. It's not far ahead. But tonight," he selected a sheltered spot under the trees, "tonight we stay put."

While he set up camp Josh talked to the animals. "Never thought I'd be so glad to see your ornery faces, cattle. Why'd you take off, anyway? Don't you *want* to get to Wyoming?" He petted Ebony's neck. "At least you had sense enough to come back."

The horse nickered and Wolf barked.

Josh laughed out loud. "It sure feels good snuggled down here for the night." He threw another log on the fire. "We'll just rest ourselves and get a good start in the morning. Hope it doesn't snow anymore."

Josh's wish came true. It didn't snow. Instead a

dense, heavy fog settled in, so thick it left everything dripping. Trees stood shrouded in the strange autumn mist. Leaves gathered the moisture then leaked it to the ground. The dampness seeped into Josh's body and crept into his spirits. How could they travel in this stuff? Why, he couldn't see more than 10 feet past the herd, and they'd come in close to the fire as if frightened of the gray world surrounding them.

"If only the North Star would show through!" He glared at the heavy sky. "We've got to get moving. Bill Mitchell and his outfit gave me enough food for what it should have taken to get us there, but now we've lost more time. Boy, if this isn't one crazy thing after another."

Suddenly he realized what he was doing and made a face. "Hey, I guess I'm as bad as those children of Israel in the Bible. No sooner did God get them out of one mess than they started complaining for fear they'd find themselves in another." With a sigh he rubbed a sooty hand across his face, leaving a black streak down his nose. Wolf grimaced at him and Josh said, "OK, OK, God's probably not going to rain manna down on us, although if He wanted to He could, but don't worry. He's out here, too." The thought made him shiver. "I wonder what it would be like to have been with Jesus? Like Peter and those guys? Wish we'd been there. I bet you wouldn't have run away when those guards came and took Jesus. I wonder if I would?" He yawned. "I s'pose it'd be easy to say no, but even Peter went back on Him, and—" Josh fell asleep.

The fog continued and the restless cattle remained close to camp. Wolf and Ebony showed no more signs of leaving. Fortunately, the bear had gone another way. But the forced inactivity took its toll on the boy. His faith wavered. When the food began to get low, fear nibbled again. He was so close and yet so far away! Pa must be with the rest of the family by now. They'd all be worried sick, his father would realize he wasn't on the trail and wouldn't know where to start looking for him.

It was only a few days until his birthday. Would he turn 13 lost on a mountainside with a bawling herd of cattle, one horse, one dog, and a God who hadn't let him down but still seemed far away in the fog?

Another morning came, dismal and discouraging. Josh couldn't stand it any longer. "Wolf, you stay on guard. Ebony, we're going to try and find the trail. The fog isn't quite so heavy." He cast a weather eye at the warning sky. Something in him whispered, *Don't go,* but he paid no attention. He couldn't stand it if he had to stay in camp any longer.

"Let's see. We headed south to find the cattle. So the trail must be north. That has to be this way." He climbed astride Ebony and started into the soft gloom.

A few hours later he let out a war whoop. "Hooray! There's the trail!" The sky had remained dark but not so much he couldn't still see. If he hurried back, he could get the herd and at least be on the main trail before night. Bill Mitchell and his friends might even cut their hunting trip short because of the weather. Josh had to be back on trail in case they did.

All went well—until his mount stepped in a gopher hole. Josh had been dozing in the saddle. He roused when Ebony went down, only to go sailing through the air over the horse's head. Then all went black.

When the boy opened his eyes he thought he'd gone blind. He felt around him. Nothing. Dazed, with an aching head, he called, "Ebony?"

A soft whinny and a cold nose on his hand was his

answer. Josh struggled to his feet. "What are we going to do now?" He could still see nothing around him.

"Can you get us back to camp, boy? Pa says give a horse his head and he'll take you home." Doubt assailed him. What if Ebony actually headed for their old home instead of for the camp? Should he stay where he was and wait until morning? He shook his head. "Ebony, take us to Wolf and the herd. Take us back to camp, old boy." Swinging into the saddle, he let the reins lie loose on the now-matted neck. A fine drizzle misted the air and turned to freezing rain.

The horse took a step, paused, then started off. Josh didn't know if it was the right direction or not. His head ached and his throat felt dry. When he lifted one hand to his head it came away sticky. He must have struck his head when he was thrown. Slumping over the saddle horn, he repeated, "Go on, Ebony. Get us to Wolf and the herd."

Comrades

Head throbbing, still a little dazed, Josh was aware of the motion of his horse's body but little else. He clung to the saddle horn, wishing he could concentrate but unable to clear his mind. At last he slipped into almost unconsciousness.

When Ebony stopped he roused. "What's wrong, old boy?"

The horse tossed his head and whinnied. Though Josh's head still hurt, he opened his eyes. The freezing rain had turned to snow. Even the murky light showed feathery flakes on Ebony's head and bridle.

Josh dug his heels into Ebony's sides, not enough to hurt him, just enough to get him going. "Don't stop now, Ebony."

When the horse refused to budge, the boy prodded him again. "What's wrong with you?"

Ebony pranced a bit but flatly refused to go on.

"Great! How can we get back to camp if you act that way?" But all his coaxing and prodding didn't move the horse from the spot he'd chosen to stop.

"Well, if you won't go, you won't go. Maybe you know something I don't." Josh sighed. "Pa always says animals are smarter than people in storms. We'll stay here. I can't haul you, that's for sure." As he fumbled in his pocket, his disgust changed to alarm. "Oh, no, the matches are in my other shirt pocket!" He stared at Ebony. "How am I going to get a fire going? It's getting colder every minute."

It was. A rush of frigid air had come with the snow. Josh clutched his jacket together, then pulled his cap low over his ears. No fire. His horse wouldn't move. Freezing weather. He could die out here maybe just a few hundred yards from camp.

Throwing his head back, he yelled, "Wolf, Wolf!"

There was no answer, not even the faint barking that would show they were anywhere near camp. Josh's heart sank again.

"The snow's muffling sounds. Well, we have to make the best of it." He looked around. Visibility was still poor, but he could see a little distance in each direction. One huge evergreen tree caught his attention. The branches bent down almost to the ground at their tips.

"I'll bet there isn't even any snow on the ground near the trunk," he told Ebony. "Come on. Let's see." He raised the heavy branches enough for the horse to follow him. Sure enough, the closely growing branches drooped back down behind him, making a wide, clear space with needle-covered ground. It was like a dry little room.

Thankfully Josh sank to the ground and rested his aching head against the massive tree trunk. "Whew! Talk about shelter. This is a dandy one." He shivered. "Now if we just had food and matches, we'd be pretty well off." As he tried to ignore his growling stomach, he said, "Wonder how Wolf's making out with the critters."

Ebony nickered and moved closer, standing in a half-resting position.

Worry crept over the boy. "It's the longest Wolf's ever had to mind the cattle. I hope he will do it. I guess we shouldn't have tried to find the trail, but Pa says a man's got to decide what to do, do it, then live with it." He yawned. "It's a lot of hours till daylight, even if the storm stops." Carefully he buttoned his coat high around his neck. "I mustn't go to sleep. I could freeze to death. Then you and Wolf and the cattle would probably all die too." Another yawn. "How am I going to keep awake all night?"

Ebony tossed his head and stamped his feet. Was he cold, too? Was he trying to show how he kept warm?

A faint memory teased at the boy's brain and slipped away. Something important. Something he should know and remember.

"Maybe I can sing." Josh forced his heavy eyelids up. He started singing everything he could remember. Fun songs, hymns, cowboy and trail songs, ballads. Still his eyelids seemed to be dragged down as if by weights.

"If only I could remember what it is that . . ." Josh slumped into sleep, but the horse's shrill neighing and pawing the ground brought him upright. His mouth stretched in a wide grin as he leaped to his feet. "That's it, Ebony! You reminded me." He drew in a great breath of cold air.

"A few years ago one of Pa's friends got caught out in a bad storm. He was on his way to a neighbor's when the snow caught him. He didn't have matches, either. He was about as bad off as we are!" He stopped for breath. "Anyway, the next day when he got to his neighbors' they were amazed and wanted to know how he could survive a blizzard.

87

"'Easy,' he said, and rubbed his legs. 'I had no choice. I couldn't go on. The only shelter I could find was a lone tree practically in the middle of nowhere. So I walked around and around it, all night long! If I'd have left it, I'd have been lost.'"

Josh began walking around the tree trunk. "Tomorrow morning I'll probably be as tired and lame as he was, but I'll be alive, Ebony. Hear that? We'll make it!"

For hours Josh circled the tree, sometimes at little more than a snail's pace. When he'd feel sleepy he'd force his feet to move faster. Other times he talked to the horse, now nodding and still.

"You know I wondered if I'd recognize when our Third Comrade helped us, Ebony?"

The horse shifted and resumed his dozing.

Josh stumbled on. "Funny. Part of the time it's been real easy to see, like Bill Mitchell finding us and our getting out of that river." Josh cringed at the memory. "Then there's been other times—the bear, and me not getting thrown against a rock and broken to pieces today. And now—remembering that story just when I needed it most. God sure works in a lot of ways, I guess, but He's been right here all the way."

Several times Josh peered through the white-covered branches. He saw when it stopped snowing, when the starlight poked through the clouds and brightened the forest. Tired but triumphant, he watched the sun rise. "Whoopee! No red sky this morning. Storm's over. Come on, Ebony, let's make tracks."

Ebony stepped out into ankle-deep snow and shook himself. Josh cupped snow in his hands so the horse could lick it and get a little water. "Now let's see why you balked last night." Mounting he retraced the

88

short distance from the tree to where they'd stopped the night before.

He stared, appalled, when the horse stopped in the same place. A few feet in front of him the ground dropped off. A sharp drop led to a deep canyon stretching below him. If Ebony hadn't sensed danger they would have gone over the edge.

For a time the boy sat speechless. Finally he said brokenly, "God, thank You for Ebony being smarter than I was. We'd have been goners." Backing the horse away from the drop-off, he turned and rode away, using the sun as a guide, absorbing its warming rays to his body and thanking God for His care in his heart.

"This is more like it," Josh said when they reached camp. The sun shone warmer today. Except for the shady patches most of the snow had started to melt. What was left was soft and easy to travel through.

The minute camp was in sight, Josh called, "Wolf?"

A joyous answering bark greeted him, but no flying feet accompanied it.

"Where are you, boy?"

Wolf barked again but still did not come out to meet them.

Josh rode into camp. "Wolf?"

Only then did the big dog leave his job and almost knock the boy over as he slid from the saddle. Red-rimmed eyes looked straight at his master.

"You look like you were up all night." Josh examined the dog carefully. He was fine except for looking tired. "I'll bet you stayed on guard just like you were told."

Wolf leaped again and barked.

"Let's count the cattle, then eat something," Josh said turning to the herd huddled together under the trees.

"Twenty-three . . . twenty-four . . . *twenty-five!*" He choked on the final number, having been almost afraid to check. "I'll say, you're a comrade for the trail, all right!" he said, spinning on his heel, his voice husky with emotion. Grabbing Wolf around the neck, he hugged him. "Hey, know what?" He stared into the furry face. "You're a steward, too! You did just what I'd have done if I'd been here. You're some dog, let me tell you."

Ebony neighed jealously and Josh ran to him. "OK, friends, let's break camp."

After all the danger and excitement they had experienced already, crossing the pass wasn't as bad as Josh had feared. Although snow covered the trail, it was not deep. A party of horsemen had gone by sometime probably the day before. "Maybe Bill Mitchell," Josh decided. "Boy, good thing we didn't count on more help from them." After herding the cattle down the eastern slope, he stopped and heaved a tremendous sigh of relief.

Below him the land sloped to the valley he knew he couldn't yet see. The going from there on would be easier. If he pushed hard and the weather held, he could probably make it to his family late the next night. Driving the cattle up the valley would be a cinch after what he'd been through so far.

The trail down from the pass was winding. Old Crumple Horn led as if he knew where he was going. Josh and Wolf and Ebony just followed along, glad for an easier day after the rough night they'd had.

Just as the sun prepared to drop out of sight, Josh saw a welcome sight. A little way ahead stood a cabin. He couldn't tell if it was deserted or if someone lived there, but it would be a good place to stop. Maybe there'd even be a bunk he could use. So far he had made good time. Tomorrow would see them finish the drive.

"No supper," he told Wolf when he found the cabin was empty. He'd shared the last bread with the dog at noon and had given Ebony the final handful of oats then, too. The herd and Ebony could find graze in the meadowlike area near the cabin, but Wolf and Josh would have to content themselves with cold water from the nearby stream.

Josh slept heavily but Wolf roused him at daylight by licking the boy's cheek with his cold tongue. "All right, all right." Josh pulled on his boots, drank some water, filled his canteen, and saw that Ebony and the herd were well watered.

A lump grew in his throat as he started the last day on the trail. The herd forged ahead now that there was a well-marked path. Ebony perked up his ears and Wolf trotted beside him.

"In spite of everything, I wouldn't have missed this." Josh thought over all the things they'd faced—fear in the night, starvation, dangers of many kinds.

"I never appreciated things before. Nothing ever tasted as good as that bread and cheese Bill Mitchell gave me, not even Ma's cooking—and it's the best! I never knew how good fire could feel until I was 'most frozen. Or water when I was thirsty. Or sleep when I was worn-out." He swallowed hard before going on. "And I never knew what animals could be like, either. Wolf, Ebony, you both saved my life."

Ebony turned to glance back at him, and Wolf pressed closer, looking up at the boy.

Josh rode on in silence, noticing how most of the

91

snow was gone. His feelings were too strong for more words. But when he topped a little rise late in the afternoon and saw a cabin, then another, he couldn't keep back a glad cry. "We're almost home!"

The herd moved faster. Ebony neighed, and another horse's shrill whistle answered. Josh would have known that sound anywhere. *"Daisy! Pa's here."*

Despite his impatience, he managed to keep himself from stampeding the herd toward that sound. Instead he concentrated on the small figures running from the cabin through a blur that persisted in getting in his eyes.

He'd made it! It had been a long way, *but he'd made it. "Twenty-three . . . twenty-four . . . twenty-five . . ."* he tallied off the herd as they spilled into the rude corral. In a minute Pa and Ma and Charity and Sam would reach him. He could see Charity's red curls bounce in the sun as she ran. But in that minute he had one more thing to do. Closing his eyes, he said, "We're here, God. There may be other drives and trails. Wolf and Ebony may not always be with me. I know now You will—and I'm glad." A rush of love raced through him. "Thank You, Third Comrade—no, *First* Comrade."

Josh closed the corral gate behind old Crumple Horn and turned to meet his family.

Date Due

MAR 1 8 2020			

BRODART, CO.   Cat. No. 23-233-003   Printed in U.S.A.